CAN YOU
HANDLE THE
TRUTH???

D0973917

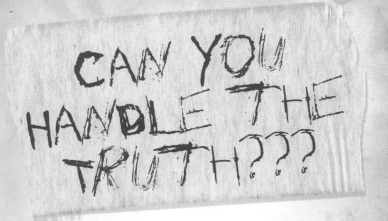

CAN YOU HANDLE THE TRUTH???

50 In-Your-Face Devotions for Teens

WRITTEN AND COMPILED BY

PHIL CHALMERS

BARBOUR

Cover design by Kirk DouPonce/www.dogeareddesign.com

Published by Barbour Publishing, Inc., P.O. Box 719,
Uhrichsville, Ohio 44683, www.barbourbooks.com

*Our mission is to publish and distribute
inspirational products offering exceptional
value and biblical encouragement to the masses.*

 Member of the
Evangelical Christian
Publishers Association

Printed in China
5 4 3 2 1

To two great people
who have had a tremendous impact
on Phil Chalmers:
Lt. Col. Robert J. Tritton,
who helped us get our start nationwide,
and Jim Hvisdos,
who helped me start True Lies in the mid-eighties.
Rest in peace, Jim!

CONTENTS

ACKNOWLEDGMENTS

Thanks to all of the writers involved, including Ron Luce, Jamie Rouse, Jim Burns, Superchic(k), Pillar, LG Wise, Doug Herman, Chrissy Rock, Tim Troyer, Jason Rose, Jonathan McKee, and Craig at XXXChurch.com. I couldn't have completed this book without you.

I also want to make it known that writers Carole Wells and Gail Carmichael were very involved in the editing of this project, and this book wouldn't be out today if it weren't for them.

Special thanks to my wife, Barb, and office manager, Leigh Ann Sterner.

Also thanks to all who have helped our ministry, including Teen Mania, Acquire the Fire, Texas Youth Commission, Christ In Youth, McCap, Interlinc, *Plugged In* magazine, Screenit.com, and our friends and family members.

Thanks to Andy Janning, Danny Holland, Brett Ullman, LG Wise, and Dean Rosson for allowing me to vent and for being my sounding board.

Thanks to the True Lies speaking team for your input, help, prayers, and support.

And most of all, thanks to Jesus Christ for allowing me to have life so I can do projects such as this. I extend my gratitude to the early Christians who gave their lives so this movement can continue and to the disciples who gave up their lives for the sake of the gospel.

introduction

I'm excited that you're reading this book. Inside you'll find a collection of powerful stories written by some of my friends and colleagues, as well as answers from the Bible on dozens of hard-hitting topics. My hope is that the testimonies and scriptural principles I've presented here will transform your life.

This resource can be used in two ways:

Study it as a fifty-day devotional. Some psychologists claim that it takes about twenty-one consecutive days to start a habit. I'm giving you fifty! Beginning right now, read a devotional entry every day, allowing the scriptures to go deep into your heart and the lessons to become a part of your daily routine. (In other words, a habit for life!)

Refer to it as a topical reference guide. Think of this as a concordance or promise book. Once you've read all of the devotions, keep this resource close by, on your nightstand, on your desk, or in your book bag. When a topic comes up, whether at school, church, or work, you can crack open the pages and have an instant story to tell, along with scripture and application. So, if someone tells you she is considering an abortion or he is contemplating suicide, you can "always be prepared to give an answer to everyone who asks you to give the reason for the hope that you have" (1 Peter 3:15).

ABOUT PHIL CHALMERS

I didn't grow up in church, and I didn't have a traditional Christian family. As a teen I was out of control, doing pretty much whatever I wanted. I was involved in sex, drugs, alcohol, violence, porn, drunk driving, as well as many other sinful activities. Through it all, I was searching for peace and purpose.

After I graduated from high school, a friend shared the message of Christ and how to gain His forgiveness and salvation. I jumped at that chance. Slowly but surely, God changed my life. Through Jesus Christ, I found the peace I was searching for, as well as God's true purpose for my life.

I started speaking to teens when I was twenty, after trying my hand at college. I've been speaking and working with teens since then, now approaching two decades. I wasn't the most talented speaker, and I'm not the best writer, but I'm proof that God can use anyone, no matter who you are. All He asks is that you are available and obedient.

FIRST THINGS FIRST

Before you get started with this devotional, let me review some basic information with you so that you can know for sure where you stand with God. It is possible to know that you have eternal life and that if you die tonight, you can be in the presence of Jesus Christ, your Creator.

STEP ONE: BECOME A CHRISTIAN

The Bible says in Romans 3:23 that "all have sinned and fall short of the glory of God," and Romans 6:23 says, "The wages of sin is death." So, all of us sin—everyone—and we have fallen short of God's standard of holiness. And because of our sin, we are getting paid a wage, which is death—physical death and spiritual death. Now, that's bad news. But there is good news! The rest of Romans 6:23 reads, "But the gift of God is eternal life in Christ Jesus our Lord." God has given us a gift—His Son. How do we receive this gift? Read on! Romans 10:9-10 says, "If you confess with your mouth 'Jesus is Lord,' and believe in your heart that God raised him from the dead, you will be saved. For it is with your heart that you believe and are justified, and it is with your mouth that you confess and are saved." Becoming a Christian involves more than just saying a magic prayer or performing lip service. You must believe in Christ's death and resurrection with your heart and confess it with your mouth. Tell someone if you have done this. Talk to your parents, a youth leader, pastor, priest, or whoever will listen. This is part of salvation.

Next, let me dispel a few misunderstandings about salvation and getting to heaven. Some people say, "I go to church, I'm a good person, and I keep the Ten Commandments." We are judged by faith, not works. What's more, it's simply not enough just to believe in God. Check out these two passages:

- Ephesians 2:8-9: "For it is by grace you have been saved, through faith—and this not from yourselves, it is the gift of God—not by works, so that no one can boast."

- James 2:19: "You believe that there is one God. Good! Even the demons believe that—and shudder."

Obviously, we know the demons are not going to heaven. The reason? Because, although they know about Jesus, they have never received Him into their lives.

Some people say a loving God would not send people to hell. And they're right, God doesn't send anyone to hell. We send ourselves to hell by rejecting Christ. And lastly, some will say that there are many ways to God. How can so many people be wrong? I'll leave you with this final thought about salvation: John 14:6, where Jesus says, "I am the way and the truth and the life. No one comes to the Father except through me."

Even after we become Christians and make Jesus the Lord of our lives, we still struggle with sin. Romans 8:1-14 talks about this battle we will have for the rest of our lives, the battle between our sinful nature (our flesh) and our spirit. Romans 8:6 says, "The mind of sinful man is death, but the mind controlled by the Spirit is life and peace." Paul talks again about the constant struggle in Romans 7:14-25. He says in verse 15, "I do not understand what I do. For what I want to do I do not do, but what I hate I do." Even though life as a Christian will not be easy, it will be worth it. We need to flee from sin and not put ourselves in positions where we can fall, like visiting a girlfriend when her parents are gone, surfing the Net when no one is around, and so on. Determine to live a blameless life—don't put yourself in a position where you can fall.

STEP THREE: ELIMINATE UNGODLY INFLUENCES

Ungodly influences include all kinds of things: friends who get into trouble, non-Christian boyfriends and girlfriends, even certain kinds of entertainment—what we put into our minds four to six hours a day. If your friends, boyfriend, or girlfriend are leading you in the wrong direction by trying to pull you away from your commitment to Christ, you need to find new friends. Now, if you can influence them, you can remain friends, but if they start influencing you, it's time to make your break.

If you choose to date, it's wise to date only Christians, as you will have something in common when making decisions about sex and the direction of your lives. A major way the enemy can take you out is through a girlfriend or boyfriend. Be careful.

When it comes to entertainment, the Bible says in Ephesians 5:1–4: "Be imitators of God, therefore, as dearly loved children and live a life of love. . . . But among you there must not be even a hint of sexual immorality, or of any kind of impurity, or of greed, because these are improper for God's holy people. Nor should there be obscenity, foolish talk or coarse joking, which are out of place." I could quote at least twenty more verses that warn us about what we listen to, watch, and put into our minds. Believe me, it does matter to God, and He makes it clear that it will affect our spiritual lives.

STEP FOUR: Find a Great Church and Youth Group

The Bible says in Hebrews 10:25, "Let us not give up meeting together, as some are in the habit of doing, but let us encourage one another—and all the more as you see the Day approaching." The Bible also talks about iron sharpening iron. It's important to be around other believers, other Christians, who can support you and with whom you have something in common. Find a good Christian friend to whom you can be accountable.

STEP FIVE: Establish a Habit of Daily Prayer, Bible Study, and Worship

Find a part of the day, perhaps morning or night, when you can pray, read the Bible, and listen to a worship song. Start out with one chapter of the New Testament per day and a cool devotional you can read—like this one. If you miss a day, don't feel guilty or beat

14

yourself up. Just begin again the next day. Soon it will become a habit, and your spiritual life will be off to a rolling start. Look at what 2 Timothy 3:15-16 has to say about God's Word, the Bible (the apostle Paul is writing to a young pastor named Timothy): "From infancy you have known the holy Scriptures, which are able to make you wise for salvation through faith in Christ Jesus. All Scripture is God-breathed and is useful for teaching, rebuking, correcting, and training in righteousness." The Bible is not just a book of man's words, but a book that God breathed so that you can learn and become wise in the things of God.

STEP SIX: BECOME AN AMBASSADOR FOR CHRIST

This is one step many people skip or don't think about. When you claim to be a Christian, suddenly people will start to watch you and your life. When I became a Christian, my whole family was watching my life, and my own parents even made fun of me for a time. One thing I learned quickly was that my life was on display, and so is yours. Second Corinthians 5:19-20 says that God "has committed to us the message of reconciliation. We are therefore Christ's ambassadors, as though God were making His appeal through us." You represent Christ to your friends, family, classmates, and relatives. You are His ambassador—always remember that. People are watching you, and you are either doing a good job as an ambassador for Christ or a bad job. We are responsible for how we live and the things we do, especially with our families and younger brothers and sisters.

If you are a parent, how you live directly affects your children. Read Luke 17:1-2 to see what happens to people who cause others to stumble: "Things that cause people to sin are bound to come, but woe to that person through whom they come.

It would be better for him to be thrown into the sea with a millstone tied around his neck than for him to cause one of these little ones to sin." That is heavy! This is why I do my best to live a holy life and not cause others to stumble.

One final verse, and this one is exciting: In 1 Timothy 4:15–16, Apostle Paul talks about how to live. He says, "Be diligent in these matters; give yourself wholly to them, so that everyone may see your progress. Watch your life and doctrine closely. Persevere in them, because if you do, you will save both yourself and your hearers." Who are your hearers? Your friends, family, classmates, and relatives. Isn't that exciting?

STEP SEVEN: BE WILLING TO DIE FOR THE CAUSE

This is where the men will separate from the boys and the women from the girls. Are you willing to be so committed to Christ that you would actually be willing to give up your life for the cause? Many before you have, and many will in the future. In America at this time, you may not be at risk of dying for your faith in Christ, but are you willing to make that kind of commitment? Instead of death, you may lose a girlfriend or boyfriend. You may become less popular at school. You may not be the homecoming king or the prom queen. There is a cost involved in making this commitment. Martin Luther King Jr. said, "If a man hasn't discovered something that he will die for, he isn't fit to live." Have you found something you are willing to die for? Is it PlayStation, Xbox, or skateboarding? How about school sports? I wouldn't die for any of those things. But Jesus Christ may be worth dying for or, at the very least, living for without compromise.

Many of the early Christians, including the apostles, had

their lives taken from them. And while they were dying, they were praying and singing hymns to their God. They understood commitment and what it meant to count the cost. I'm asking you to count the cost, as well. When Andrew, Peter's brother and an apostle, was being led to his cross to die, he said, "O cross, most welcome and long looked for" *(Foxe's Book of Martyrs)*. Matthew was killed with a spear. Philip was crucified and stoned to death. James, the brother of Jesus, who at first didn't believe Jesus was God or that He rose from the dead, was thrown off of a temple but survived. When he hit the ground, he turned on his knees, asking God to forgive those who tried to take his life. They ended up beating him on the head with a heavy instrument to kill him. The apostle Peter was crucified upside down at his own request, because he said he was unworthy to die like Jesus. The apostle Paul was killed by a sword put to his neck.

The stories continue. I would highly recommend you read *Foxe's Book of Martyrs*. It will really encourage you in your walk with God. The stories of early Christians are amazing. They will give you strength and encouragement to be bolder and to be more committed to what God has called you to do.

Let me leave you with one final scripture before you start this devotional. In Mark 8:34–36 Jesus says, "If anyone would come after me, he must deny himself and take up his cross and follow me. For whoever wants to save his life will lose it, but whoever loses his life for me and for the gospel will save it. What good is it for a man to gain the whole world, yet forfeit his soul?" Be encouraged, be strong, and go live your life as God would have you live it, and people will be drawn to Christ not by what you say, but by how you live.

PHIL CHALMERS, True Lies founder
Graduate of the "School of Hard Knocks"

abortion
SARA GRIVAS

Here I am again. Why did I let this happen? I'm pregnant for the third time—and still no wedding ring. I'm older, wiser, and I know the hardships of raising a child on my own. I don't know if I'm able to face the disappointment of my parents—*again*. I'm so embarrassed. What about my education? My career? My future is once again put on hold. Oh, the gossip and judgment are only going to make my guilt and shame so much more unbearable. The only way I can face them again is if they don't know. How can I get out of this situation? How can I make it all go away? What have other women done when faced with this dilemma?

One week later. It all happened so quickly. Supposedly, the only cost was the $250 fee I paid up front. After a brief "informational" session with three other girls, I was led to a cold, dark room. I was scared as I lay there on a long table. I tried to convince myself that I was doing the right thing as the chills ran up and down my body. There was no one there to hold my hand, no one to comfort me, no one to say that everything would be okay. There was no one to wipe the tears that slowly streamed down my face as I literally had the life sucked out of me. The only thing I heard was the horrifying sound of the "human vacuum" and the chilling voice of the doctor continually reminding me to relax as my knees naturally buckled closed.

My mind was racing as I fought my body into submission. I was overwhelmed as the frustrated doctor said, "Listen! You've already had two births. Quit being such a baby! You're making this way too hard for me!" At that moment, all the fight in me left. My body became limp, and I gave up. It was as if I were dead but still breathing. I walked out of that building bleeding, empty, and hollow.

I carry that same lonely feeling with me every day. The embarrassment that I was trying to avoid that day has turned into a life of guilt and shame of a mother who "chose" to kill her own child. The cost was much more than $250. I walked into that building with life and walked out with death. Two people died that day—both by my own choice.

To this day I wonder what my child would have looked like. What will he or she say to me in heaven? Oh, how I yearn to hold the child I chose to kill. I'd give anything to say, "I'm sorry."

People try to justify abortion. They argue over rights and definitions of life. Many try to find a middle ground and say abortion is acceptable if a woman is raped. I'm very happy that a fifteen-year-old Michigan girl didn't take that advice after she had been raped. She chose adoption for her baby girl who grew up to be one of the most compassionate abstinence speakers in the country, Pam Stenzel. Even though Pam has never met her biological mother, she is very grateful that she chose life for her. Her story proves that there is a better option when faced with an unwanted pregnancy—life.

WHAT DOES GOD SAY???

God is perfectly clear on this issue—it's black and white. Exodus 20:13 and Deuteronomy 5:17 make it plain: "You shall not murder." There is no option; you are not to kill your own child. If I could go back in time, I would accept the few short months of shame and guilt of being pregnant outside of marriage. I'm living proof that shame fades with time. I had a child at a very young age—before I was married. That temporary embarrassment is much easier to live with than the pain of losing a child—a pain I still carry with me to this day.

Is it really a child?

> *"Before I formed you in the womb I knew you,*
> *before you were born I set you apart."*
>
> Jeremiah 1:5

> *For you created my inmost being;*
> *you knit me together in my mother's womb.*
>
> Psalm 139:13

> *I praise you because I am fearfully and*
> *wonderfully made; your works are wonderful,*
> *I know that full well. My frame was not hidden*
> *from you when I was made in the secret place.*
> *When I was woven together in the depths of the*
> *earth, your eyes saw my unformed body.*
> *All the days ordained for me were written in*
> *your book before one of them came to be.*
>
> Psalm 139:14-16

What if I've already had an abortion? Will God forgive me?

> *If we confess our sins, he is faithful and*
> *just and will forgive us our sins and purify*
> *us from all unrighteousness.*
>
> 1 John 1:9

> *When you were dead in your sins and in the*
> *uncircumcision of your sinful nature, God*
> *made you alive with Christ. He forgave us all*
> *our sins, having canceled the written code,*
> *with its regulations, that was against us and*
> *that stood opposed to us; he took it away,*
> *nailing it to the cross.*
>
> Colossians 2:13-14

How should we treat someone when we discover she has had an abortion?

> "My command is this: Love each other as I have loved you."
>
> JOHN 15:12

HOW DOES THIS AFFECT ME???

Two wrongs don't make a right. Keep in mind that abortion is not a solution to a "problem." It won't fix anything! The only real solution is to offer the best possible life for the child. You have two options: (1) Keep the child and raise him or her in a stable family environment—preferably with both a mother and father; (2) Put your baby up for adoption. There are many reliable Christian adoption agencies that represent loving, solid families who have a lot to offer. Remember, there are always consequences for your actions. If you have an abortion, you can be forgiven, but you will have to live with the consequences of that decision for the rest of your life.

SARA GRIVAS is a True Lies speaker. To contact abstinence speaker Pam Stenzel, check out her Web site at www.PamStenzel.com.

abuse and molestation

LEE RUST

My grandpa was a large man with big hands and a tall, lean body. Actually, he was my third grandfather by age four. I can't say that I remember much about him until I was close to nine. He took an interest in me and spoke to me as if I were "a big girl." He would ask me to help him with all sorts of things, like shaving his beard with an electric razor or clipping his toenails. He made me feel so grown up when he asked me to perform these personal hygiene tasks. Even though he was in his early seventies, he always seemed eager for my visits.

It was great for a while, but then he began asking me for kisses that lasted longer and longer each time. He would grab and touch my body. I hated it, but I didn't know what to do. He eventually started luring me to the yard away from Grandma. He would invite me to sit in his lap. He never acted like it was wrong or bad as he continued to sexually molest me. Sometimes he even exposed himself to me at night after my Grandma had gone to sleep. He frightened me, and I no longer wanted to spend the night at my grandparents' home, but I was afraid to tell anyone.

Years later, after my grandfather had passed away, I found the courage to tell my mom. In her shock, she accused me of lying. I guess it was easier for her to deal with a child who was a liar than face the reality of my grandfather's actions.

I'm reminded almost daily of the injustice against my innocent, unknowing frame. My childhood was spent in fear and shame. Unfortunately, once the cycle began, I fell victim to other men and abusers during my childhood. Even though I became a Christian at the age of twelve, my past had tainted my understanding of love. I grew into a young woman who had no clear picture of how true love looked, acted, or felt.

I trusted no one. I had been abused mentally, physically, and sexually by those closest to me—my own family members. I couldn't seem to break free. When I got married, my husband was an abuser. I lived my nightmare for seven more years. Then I called out to God and submitted my entire life and heart to Him. He delivered me from this horrible life, and I began to trust God in ways I had never imagined. I speak with Him every morning, and He guides me through the day as I continue to learn how to love and trust for the first time in my life.

WHAT DOES GOD SAY???

Abuse, in many forms, is addressed throughout God's Word. He wants to warn, protect, and help us in our daily lives. The first thing I had to learn was that God loves *me*! This was very difficult because I had never known unconditional love. Second, I had to realize that the abuse was not my fault. As a result, my guilt was released.

If you or someone you know is struggling with a similar past (or present), here is what the Bible has to say:

> The LORD is close to the brokenhearted and
> saves those who are crushed in spirit.
>
> > PSALM 34:18

> He will cover you with his feathers, and
> under his wings you will find refuge; his
> faithfulness will be your shield and rampart
> [a defense].
>
> > PSALM 91:4

Be still before the LORD and wait patiently
for him; do not fret when men succeed in
their ways, when they carry out their wicked
schemes. Refrain from anger and turn from
wrath; do not fret—it leads only to evil. For
evil men will be cut off, but those who hope
in the LORD will inherit the land.

PSALM 37:7-9

For the verse below, insert your name in place of "the world." God loves *you*!

"God so loved the world that he gave his one
and only Son, that whoever believes in him
shall not perish but have eternal life."

JOHN 3:16

God's plan doesn't include abuse. If you are being abused, tell someone today, and take action. There are people who can help you. E-mail me or Phil Chalmers for help.

"For I know the plans I have for you," declares
the LORD, "plans to prosper you and not to harm
you, plans to give you hope and a future."

JEREMIAH 29:11

Let me assure you, something good can come from being abused or molested. Perhaps someone needs your help.

We know that in all things God works for the
good of those who love him, who have been
called according to his purpose.

ROMANS 8:28

HOW DOES THIS AFFECT ME???

Have you been mistreated in some way? If so, tell someone. If that person doesn't believe you, tell someone else. Keep speaking out until the truth is known. God loves you and does not desire this kind of harm to come to you. He is a loving and just God.

When I decided to let God handle my life, things got better. It was a new day. Break the cycle. Avoid others who will only abuse and harm you; turn to God for love, protection, wisdom, and guidance. I can safely say that God can heal you if you are hurting. He has taken every aspect of my abuse as a child and an adult and used it to glorify His name. I am now married to a wonderful, godly man who loves and cares for me in a healthy relationship. I pray you will not wait as long as I did to begin a trust relationship with God.

Today I am the founder of Freedom Forever Ministries, which teaches life skills to female inmates in county jail systems. I share God's abundant love and understanding with incarcerated women—90 percent of whom have been abused. God continues to bring healing every time I teach a class. I never dreamed that I would be the one He would choose for this task. But then again, I've walked in their shoes and lived with the same shame and guilt. I'm so thankful that God has chosen to heal and transform my broken life into a vessel for His message.

LEE RUST is the founder of Freedom Forever Ministries. Have questions? E-mail her at elrust@vci.net.

accountability

LONNY HARPER

Coach Marinello spent more time with the guys on his football team than most of their parents did. They were together from the last school bell until the sun went down. Their days were filled with practice, game tapes, strategy meetings, and workouts that all led up to the big Friday night game each week. They sweated, bled, cried, and celebrated together.

As they rode the ups and downs of high school football, the players on the team learned that Coach Marinello was the real deal. He admitted his struggles, shortcomings, and pain. As the bond between coach and players grew, they also learned he was a man they could trust. They would seek out his advice when they were having a hard time.

Coach knew what they needed. He gathered the players around and taught them about accountability. This was a new concept to many of the young men. Soon many of the guys on the team began to develop small groups of three, four, or five guys whom they trusted the most. They started meeting at lunch just to talk "guy to guy." As the rest of the school chowed down on pizza and soda, these guys were beginning to understand how to be true friends. As trust grew, they began to open up and ask each other tough questions. Their friendship grew as they prayed for each other every day. They soon realized that they were much stronger together than they had been alone.

We all need accountability. King David was one of the great men of God in the Bible. As the king of Israel, he led his nation to countless victories. After winning so many battles, as well as the hearts of his people, he began to believe in his own strength. As king he was accountable to no one. So when he spotted the beautiful Bathsheba bathing, he was tempted. His temptation led to a sexual encounter with the married woman, resulting in adultery.

In David's attempt to cover his tracks, he also became guilty of murder by having Bathsheba's husband killed in battle. Imagine how the story could have been different had King David been accountable to someone. His male counterpart would have known this weakness and possibly could have helped prevent this tragedy. Consider what the Bible says about accountability.

Why do I need accountability?

Above all else, guard your heart.

PROVERBS 4:23

If you think you are standing firm, be careful that you don't fall!

1 CORINTHIANS 10:12

Two are better than one, because they have a good return for their work: If one falls down, his friend can help him up. But pity the man who falls and has no one to help him up! Also, if two lie down together, they will keep warm. But how can one keep warm alone?
Though one may be overpowered, two can defend themselves. A cord of three strands is not quickly broken.

ECCLESIASTES 4:9-12

I want accountability. How do I get it?

> *Confess your sins to each other and pray for each other so that you may be healed. The prayer of a righteous man is powerful and effective.*

JAMES 5:16

HOW DOES THIS AFFECT ME???

We all need accountability. By God's design, we all make up the body of Christ, the church. If your eyes decide they don't want to do their job, the rest of your body is going to suffer. In the same way, if you don't do your part in the body of Christ, we all suffer. We must rely on each other to grow and function in the way Jesus intended. We need one another.

I challenge you to find accountability partners. Choose people of the same gender whom you respect. Find people with whom you feel compatible and whose judgment you trust. Determine to meet once a week and pray for each other daily. When you do get together, spend your time doing the following:

1. Share your struggles and triumphs.
2. Ask each other tough questions (confess your sins).
3. Pray for each other.

Spend your time together encouraging, strengthening, and learning from one another. This relationship must be built upon trust and honesty. If not, you are wasting your time. You can only help and pray for one another if you all are honest about your daily struggles.

LONNY HARPER is a youth speaker.

alcohol

DANNY HOLLAND

What's so bad about having a drink or two? Is it really that big of a deal? Well, yes, it can be. Alcohol is the leading cause of death for teenagers. It is a factor in 80 percent of all family violence. And it can justify to the mind of an impaired driver behind the wheel of an out-of-control vehicle that he or she is fit to drive. This highly accessible legal drug is often abused. A casual indulgence can lead to a lifelong addiction.

Even though drinking is a personal decision, it inevitably affects others. An alcohol-induced haze can impair judgment and cause you to harm your family, friends, or even strangers. Just ask Jacqueline Saburido. As she innocently drove along, she was struck by a drunk teenager driving an SUV. Her car burst into flames as she struggled for her life. As a result, over 60 percent of her body suffered third-degree burns and she was disfigured. Jacqueline's story is only one example of the thousands of drunk driving accidents that occur every year.

Alcohol is a large fixture in our culture. Television, movies, and even our friends make it seem like everyone drinks. But that's not accurate. Most teenagers think, *They'll think I'm lying when I tell them that I have never had a drink of alcohol in my life.* Yet it is possible to live your entire life without experimenting with alcohol.

You wouldn't believe how many times fellow Christians have asked me, "Is it okay for me to drink alcohol?" That's a good question but not the *right* one. As we turn to God's Word for guidance, we quickly learn that it is not a list of rules. It leads us to a closer walk with God. It encourages us to seek Him first—not just get by, by following a bunch of rules. God did not

sacrifice His only Son so He could come to earth to play umpire.
Jesus came to us, walked with us, and lived a human life so He
could invite us into relationship with Him. The Bible is a love
letter from God. It reveals His love, His sacrifice, and His desire
to be close to us.

WHAT DOES GOD SAY???

God's Word offers example after example of actions we can take
that will bring us closer or further away from Him. Alcohol is
directly mentioned. The Bible tells us clearly that those who get
drunk will not enter heaven.

The following verses were written to church attendees.

> *Neither. . .thieves nor the greedy nor*
> *drunkards nor slanderers nor swindlers will*
> *inherit the kingdom of God.*
>
> 1 CORINTHIANS 6:9-10

> *The acts of the sinful nature are obvious. . .*
> *envy; drunkenness, orgies, and the like. I*
> *warn you, as I did before, that those who live*
> *like this will not inherit the kingdom of God.*
>
> GALATIANS 5:19-21

In the Old Testament, leaders such as Moses and Aaron were given
specific times and conditions to abstain from alcohol.

> *Then the LORD said to Aaron, "You and your sons*
> *are not to drink wine or other fermented drink*
> *whenever you go into the Tent of Meeting, or*
> *you will die. This is a lasting ordinance for*
> *the generations to come. You must distinguish*

between the holy and the common, between the unclean and the clean, and you must teach the Israelites all the decrees the LORD has given them through Moses."

LEVITICUS 10:8-11

The LORD said to Moses, "Speak to the Israelites and say to them: 'If a man or woman wants to make a special vow, a vow of separation to the LORD as a Nazirite, he must abstain from wine and other fermented drink and must not drink vinegar made from wine or from other fermented drink.' "

NUMBERS 6:1-3

HOW DOES THIS AFFECT ME???

So what's the "right" question? Try asking yourself, "What can I avoid or remove from my life to please God more?" Alcohol may be that thing. If God is leading you away from it, then you have to decide which is more important—your relationship with the Creator or a temporary high.

Remember, as a Christian you are called to live a life acceptable to God—not one based on cultural norms. It may be "acceptable" to drink in our culture, but we must remember that God told us we are foreigners in this land, and according to the Bible, we should not conform to the patterns of this world that would distance us from God. But where is the line? When are we supposed to be part of this world and when are we to be separate? If you're ever confused or frustrated, just go to God and ask for His guidance. He will give it. But be prepared to listen and take action with His answer. No matter the topic, God wants us to seek Him first and then obey. This is the foundation of a growing relationship with God.

So did I miss out by not drinking alcohol? Only on possible regrets, addiction, and pain. I have had great relationships, fulfilling jobs, and a lot of fun in my life—with no regrets! I would like to challenge you to join me in living an alcohol-free life.

DANNY HOLLAND is the True Lies executive director.

anger

ROGER PALMER

5

There probably isn't a soul on earth who hasn't gotten angry
and lost his or her cool with someone. For you, maybe it was your
little sister who caused you to blow your top. Maybe it was a bully
at school, a rude driver, or someone who took a cheap shot at you
during a ball game. Whatever the case, you're not alone. We all
were created with a wide variety of emotions, including anger. This
God-given emotion can easily be misused if left out of check.

I vividly remember a time when my anger got the best of me.
I was a freshman in college, not yet a Christian, and having a
difficult time with my girlfriend. As one of my buddies and I
were driving around one day, he began to ask me questions about
my relationship with my girlfriend. I began to explain our
problems, feeling the anger stacking up inside of me. The more I
talked, the angrier I got. My animated personality came out as
I began swinging my arms to express my frustration. Suddenly I
found myself taking a punch at the windshield. The next thing
I knew, it shattered into a giant spiderweb design. We both sat
there in total shock. Soon we were able to laugh about the
ridiculous situation.

When your anger is left unchecked, you can end up doing
something really foolish. For me, it was the cost of a windshield.
What has your anger cost you?

WHAT DOES GOD SAY???

We should listen first and think before speaking or getting
angry.

My dear brothers, take note of this: Everyone should be quick to listen, slow to speak and slow to become angry, for man's anger does not bring about the righteous life that God desires.

JAMES 1:19-20

Before we get angry, we should ask for wisdom.

If any of you lacks wisdom, he should ask God, who gives generously to all without finding fault, and [wisdom] will be given to him.

JAMES 1:5

Know that even Jesus got angry, yet He didn't sin. Take care of the situation, forgive, and move on. If not, Satan will start to work in the situation.

"In your anger do not sin": Do not let the sun go down while you are still angry, and do not give the devil a foothold.

EPHESIANS 4:26-27

HOW DOES THIS AFFECT ME???

The next time you enter a situation that you feel is going to make you angry, be quick to listen and slow to speak, and ask God to help you judge the situation "rightly." You may be surprised to see how little there is to be angry about.

ROGER PALMER is a True Lies speaker.

25

bullying

TONY BRACKEMYRE

Bullies are everywhere. There're in your school, at your work, even hanging out at the park. At some point, everyone has been hurt or humiliated by a bully's words or fists. If you've fallen victim to a neighborhood thug, let me offer you a little insight. Not about the bully and why he or she behaves this way, but about the bigger picture of life. As you find yourself on the receiving end of someone else's anger, remember all of those who have gone before you. For example, Erika Harold—the 2003 Miss America. That's right! When she was in the ninth grade, Erika was constantly harassed by other students. They made up songs that put her down, called her a loser, and told her that she wasn't pretty. Some even vandalized her home and threatened her life. "I will never forget what it felt like to be made to feel that I wasn't good enough, that I wasn't valuable," she says.

You may think that Erika's experience is unique. Not exactly. Many successful, powerful, wealthy, and beautiful adults have their own stories of bullies from their childhood. Frank Peretti—the successful author of several popular books, including *This Present Darkness* and *Piercing the Darkness*—was a victim. In his book *The Wounded Spirit*, Peretti shares what his childhood was like. "I'm close to fifty years of age, but I still remember the names and I can see the faces of those individuals who made my life a living hell day after day after day during my childhood. I remember their words, their taunts, their blows, their spittle, and their humiliations. As I review my life, I think of all the decisions I shied away from, all the risks I dared not take, all the questions I never asked, all the relationships I didn't pursue simply because I didn't want to hurt again."

When you're feeling beaten down by the harsh hand of a bully, remember that you are just another success story waiting to be written. What's your passion? Your talent? Whatever it is, find it, pursue it, and always remember the bigger picture. Life is bigger than the here and now.

WHAT DOES GOD SAY???

Our Creator has a lot to say about you. Take a moment to look into the mirror of God's Word to get a clear reflection of who you really are.

"The LORD does not look at the things man looks at. Man looks at the outward appearance, but the LORD looks at the heart."

1 SAMUEL 16:7

You see, at just the right time, when we were still powerless, Christ died for the ungodly. Very rarely will anyone die for a righteous man, though for a good man someone might possibly dare to die. But God demonstrates his own love for us in this: while we were still sinners, Christ died for us.

ROMANS 5:6-8

What, then, shall we say in response to this? If God is for us, who can be against us? He who did not spare his own Son, but gave him up for us all—how will he not also, along with him, graciously give us all things?

ROMANS 8:31-32

This is how God showed his love among us: He sent his one and only Son into the world that we might live through him. This is love: not that we loved God, but that he loved us and sent his Son as an atoning sacrifice for our sins. Dear friends, since God so loved us, we also ought to love one another. No one has ever seen God; but if we love one another, God lives in us and his love is made complete in us.

1 JOHN 4:9-12

HOW DOES THIS AFFECT ME???

Are you being bullied? Erika Harold was picked on because of her racial background. Frank Peretti was singled out because he had a medical condition. Maybe you get picked on because you are too tall, too short, too thin, or too big. But remember that you are God's special creation. You have been wonderfully made in His image. Step back, see the bigger picture, and press forward with your own success story. In the meantime, talk to someone. Not just a buddy, but a trusted adult, such as a teacher, principal, youth leader, or parent. You can find a lot of reinforcement in the success stories of those around you.

If you find yourself on the other side, there's healing for you, too. Ask yourself why you pick on others. Is it purely peer pressure? Do you like the rush? Or are you just ticked off about something in your own life? No matter the reason, it is unacceptable! Find a way to deal with your own issues, and stop taking it out on those around you. Because we all are God's creation, we deserve respect.

TONY BRACKEMYRE is a True Lies speaker.

christian music

BRAD TAYLOR

with PHIL CHALMERS

I love music! There seems to be a song, sound, or instrument that fits every emotion. As a young Christian, I went through a process of evaluating everything in my life. I began to eliminate all different kinds of sin—porn, sex, drugs, alcohol, violence, and partying. But I had trouble releasing my choice in music. It was the mid-eighties, and I was really into bands like AC/DC, KISS, Def Leppard, Poison, and Mötley Crüe. I knew that their message wasn't exactly supporting the life I was trying to live. A Christian friend offered me a Sandi Patty album as an alternative. Sandi Patty may be talented, but her music wasn't even close to the type of music I loved.

Then one day I tuned in a Christian radio station and heard some really cool music. These guys were singing about Christ, but their sound rocked. I thought, *Christian rock does exist!* It had the same great, full, bass-driven sound that I was used to. It was a little difficult to find these albums in stores, but it was well worth the effort. I found myself special ordering certain CDs just to get what I was looking for.

Discovering Christian rock made a huge difference in my daily life. This was the type of music I loved, and they were singing about the God I was learning to love. No more satanic, violent, or sexual messages. I actually related to these artists.

So what are you listening to? Does it bring you closer to God? Would you be embarrassed if Jesus walked in the door as you sang the lyrics? Don't compromise your spiritual walk just because you like a guitar rift or the lead singer is really hot. There's a better alternative. Check out some Christian artists—and not just the ones on the radio station your mom listens to.

WHAT DOES GOD SAY???

God wants believers to encourage one another with Christian music.

> *Speak to one another with psalms, hymns and spiritual songs. Sing and make music in your heart to the Lord, always giving thanks to God the Father for everything, in the name of our Lord Jesus Christ.*
>
> EPHESIANS 5:19-20

God wants His people to fill their minds with the things of God, not of the world or the enemy.

> *Finally, brothers, whatever is true, whatever is noble, whatever is right, whatever is pure, whatever is lovely, whatever is admirable—if anything is excellent or praiseworthy—think about such things.*
>
> PHILIPPIANS 4:8

> *See to it that no one takes you captive through hollow and deceptive philosophy, which depends on human tradition and the basic principles of this world rather than on Christ.*
>
> COLOSSIANS 2:8

God wants to be praised.

> *Praise him with the sounding of the trumpet, praise him with the harp and lyre, praise him with tambourine and dancing, praise him with the strings and flute, praise him with the*

clash of cymbals, praise him with resounding
cymbals. Let everything that has breath praise
the LORD.

PSALM 150:3-6

Stop allowing yourself to be deceived. God commands us to stay away from any hint of sex, violence, or obscenity.

But among you there must not be even a hint
of sexual immorality, or of any kind of
impurity, or of greed, because these are
improper for God's holy people. Nor should
there be obscenity, foolish talk or coarse
joking, which are out of place, but rather
thanksgiving. . . . Let no one deceive
you with empty words, for because of such
things God's wrath comes on those who are
disobedient. Therefore do not be partners
with them.

EPHESIANS 5:3-4, 6-7

HOW DOES THIS AFFECT ME???

"Alternative" isn't the best way to describe Christian music. It is not a deviation from the norm. Actually, God is the creator and orchestrator of music. We are meant to sing, play, share, pray, praise, struggle, and worship through music. There are a lot of options out there. Make wise choices.

For a list of Christian bands and the mainstream bands they are similar to, log on to www.TrueLies.org, and look for the positive comparison chart.

*BRAD TAYLOR is a True Lies youth speaker.
The opening story is by Phil Chalmers.*

41

condemnation

KJ-52

I'm a rap artist with Uprok Records. My style is similar to Eminem—
otherwise known as Slim Shady. At first it bothered me when people
would compare my music to Eminem. But one night I was approached
by a fan who told me my music made a difference in his life. He began
to listen to my raps solely because they reminded him of Eminem. I
was humbled. I soon realized that my calling was to reach the lost
who were caught up in violent or depressing music.

The more I thought about it, I asked myself, "What if I wrote
Eminem a letter? What would I say? Better yet, what would Jesus
want him to know?" Thus, after two very late-night writing
sessions, "Dear Slim" was birthed, and the rest is history.

Even though I wrote "Dear Slim" to Eminem, the message
behind the song goes way beyond my drafting a response to Slim
Shady. The song is about God's heartbeat for the lost and those
living outside His love.

Songwriting is a lot like writing letters and poems. As
a teenager I loved to write love letters to girls. Some girls
wouldn't even open the envelopes. Yet others would cherish the
letters. When people ignore God's letters, He must feel something
like I felt when my letters were ignored. In the Bible, He has
given us sixty-six different books that are full of His love and
guidance for our lives. They share the actions and sacrifice of
Jesus. They tell the story of His life on earth and how He cried
out, "I love you," with every drop of blood He shed.

The Bible is truly the greatest love letter known to humankind. Today most people have heard this love letter, some over
and over. It's not enough just to hear it. You have to make
a decision about what you'll do with the message of love it

contains. What will you do with God's love letter?

WHAT DOES GOD SAY???

If you are a Christian, you don't ever have to feel condemned.

> *Therefore, there is now no condemnation for those who are in Christ Jesus.*
>
> ROMANS 8:1

We must speak to people in love, not condemnation. Saying, "You're going to hell unless you repent, sinner," is not a good way to communicate God's love for the lost.

> *Instead, [speak] the truth in love.*
>
> EPHESIANS 4:15

Be sure not to judge your brother or you, too, will be judged.

> *"Do not judge, or you too will be judged. For in the same way you judge others, you will be judged, and with the measure you use, it will be measured to you."*
>
> MATTHEW 7:1-2

HOW DOES THIS AFFECT ME???

Why should we love people like Eminem? One of the greatest responses I get back from my song is that I inspire others to look at those like Eminem in a different light. My song was never written to make Eminem the enemy or to paint him as the cause of the downfall of society. We have all fallen short of the glory of God. We may not like what he raps about and may even hate his message, but we are to love him.

God called us to love the unlovable. People will respond to practical love. Jesus' life is a perfect example of love in action, and we should follow in His steps. We are called to love the sinner but hate the sin, so find a sinner to love, and show him or her the love of Christ through your actions, not just your words.

KJ-52 is a popular Christian rap artist. To find out more about his ministry and music, log on to www.KJ52.com.

dating
PHIL CHALMERS

As I shared in the introduction, I didn't grow up as a Christian kid, so I had no idea that there was such a thing as Christian dating. If only I had read a book like this in high school, I might not have messed up so badly.

I started going out with girls when I was in junior high school. I had only two goals in mind: to date the hottest "chicks" I could possibly date and to score with as many of them as I possibly could. Unfortunately, I was somewhat successful at both.

It wasn't that hard. You see, I was a football player and had been successful in a few weightlifting tournaments. So all I had to do was play the cool, tough guy. As a result, I dated a lot of cheerleaders and hot chicks. If I only wanted to have a good time, I would pursue one of the "bad girls" who were into partying. All of my friends were doing the same thing. We celebrated each other's victories. I'm embarrassed to think about how we stole the innocence of many young ladies. We had never been taught that these "chicks" we were taking advantage of were actually young women. They were someone's daughters, someone's sisters, and someone's future wife. What a mistake!

WHAT DOES GOD SAY???

You can't find a book of the Bible dedicated to dating guidelines, because people didn't date during the time it was written. Marriages were prearranged, and there was no need for courtship. But the Bible does have clear principles that apply to dating and finding a future spouse.

You will become what your friends are. That includes your boyfriend or girlfriend.

> *Do not be misled: "Bad company corrupts good character."*
>
> 1 Corinthians 15:33

You should *never* date an unbeliever.

> *Do not be yoked together with unbelievers. For what do righteousness and wickedness have in common? Or what fellowship can light have with darkness?*
>
> 2 Corinthians 6:14

You must steer clear from sexual immorality or fornication, and remain pure until marriage. How? By practicing self-control and reading God's Word.

> *But among you there must not be even a hint of sexual immorality, or of any kind of impurity, or of greed, because these are improper for God's holy people.*
>
> Ephesians 5:3

> *It is God's will that you should be sanctified: that you should avoid sexual immorality; that each of you should learn to control his own body in a way that is holy and honorable, not in passionate lust like the heathen, who do not know God; and that in this matter no one should wrong his brother or take advantage of him. The Lord will punish men for all such sins, as we have already told you and warned you. For God did not call us to be impure, but to live a holy life. Therefore, he who rejects this instruction does not reject man but God, who gives you his Holy Spirit.*
>
> 1 Thessalonians 4:3-8

How can a young man keep his way pure? By living according to your word.
I seek you with all my heart; do not let me stray from your commands.
I have hidden your word in my heart that I might not sin against you.

PSALM 119:9-11

As always, you must honor and obey your parents. Believe it or not, they have been down this path before you.

"Honor your father and your mother, so that you may live long in the land the LORD your God is giving you."

EXODUS 20:12

HOW DOES THIS AFFECT ME???

What I'm about to drop on you may be a bit shocking to some—or at least a new way of thinking. If you date outside of the biblical foundations listed above, you are headed down the wrong path. As with the rest of your life, ignoring God's principles will only lead to pain and regret.

It is unlikely that any person you date during your teenage years will become your lifelong spouse. Just because you are attracted to the opposite sex doesn't mean that you are ready to engage in dating.

So here is my recommendation: Seriously consider not dating until you are sixteen. If you like someone of the opposite sex, try group dating. Go to the movies, bowling, or putt-putt golf with a group of friends. This will help you avoid the pressure of physical contact. Once you turn sixteen, consider double dating or small group dating. It is a safe and fun way to remain pure and accountable. As you grow older, you will begin to seek out dating partners based on the qualities you are looking for in a future spouse and not just the best-looking or coolest guy/girl around.

Regardless of the situation, protect your virginity. Believe it or not, it is special. God designed sex to be a very intimate connection shared for a lifetime between a husband and wife. There is more of life to be lived; don't blow it on a moment of fleeting passion.

PHIL CHALMERS is the founder of True Lies Youth Talks.

PHIL CHALMERS

Death is tough to think about. Eventually we all have to deal with the pain of loss, whether the loss of a family member, friend, or stranger. Death is one of the consequences of living in a fallen world. Before Adam and Eve sinned, there was no death, no separation from God. Thankfully, God has made a way for us to be reunited with Him spiritually. But we are still faced with the pain of physical death.

I experienced such pain when a friend lost his battle with colon cancer. His name was Jim Hvisdos, and he was the first kid I ever had in a youth group. Later we started the True Lies ministry together. We traveled across the country in a pickup truck, helping and loving hundreds of teens along the way. We may have driven, slept, and eaten in a truck, but we felt the leading of God through it all.

Before long, Jim left for Bible school and was later hired by a church in California. We didn't communicate much during those five years—just an occasional telephone call or visit. When I would travel to California, we would get together and have a burger and reminisce about old times.

One October Jim made a surprise visit to my home in Ohio with his girlfriend. She was a fine young lady, and we all heard marriage bells in the near future.

Unfortunately, Jim never had the chance to propose to or marry his first love. He didn't even have the opportunity to watch the graduation of his middle school students. The thirty-four-year-old man was diagnosed with colon cancer that Thanksgiving. We buried him two months later.

But this story has a happy ending. Jim was a man of God, and he was ready to meet his Creator. Most of us take life for granted, but the truth is, all of our days are numbered, and every day we live is a gift from God. When I wake up in the morning, I thank God for another day. I pray you will live your life the same way, prepared to meet God today, yet hopeful to serve Him here tomorrow.

WHAT DOES GOD SAY???

The easiest way to describe death is as a separation. Our physical death is merely a separation of our body from our spirit. But spiritual death is separation from God for eternity. When you are born again, you will die only a physical death. You will never again be separated from God—even in death. I love the saying "When you are born once, you die twice; when you are born twice, you die only once." (See John 11:25–26; Revelation 20:14.)

Why do we die? We die because sin entered the world through Adam and Eve.

> Just as sin entered the world through one man, and death through sin, and in this way death came to all men, because all sinned.
>
> ROMANS 5:12

> For the wages of sin is death, but the gift of God is eternal life through Christ Jesus our Lord.
>
> ROMANS 6:23

What happens after we die? We face judgment.

> Man is destined to die once, and after that to face judgment.
>
> HEBREWS 9:27

Should we fear death? Not if we know Christ in a personal way.

> Even though I walk through the valley of the shadow of death, I will fear no evil, for you are with me; your rod and your staff, they comfort me.
>
> PSALM 23:4

> "Where, O death, is your victory? Where, O death, is your sting?" The sting of death is sin, and the power of sin is the law. But thanks be to God! He gives us the victory through our Lord Jesus Christ.
>
> 1 CORINTHIANS 15:55-57

HOW DOES THIS AFFECT ME???

Know the facts. You will physically die unless you experience the second coming of Christ in your lifetime. Our time is short, so be prepared to meet God. Stay close and serve Him with passion. And most of all, don't fear death. Just think, it's the same day that you will bow in the mighty presence of the Lord!

PHIL CHALMERS is the founder of True Lies Youth Talks.

depression

ANDY JANNING

Imagine feeling so hopeless and empty inside—so paralyzed with sadness—that you can't even muster up the strength to crawl out of bed. You catch a glimpse of yourself in a mirror and cringe. *Why would anyone like me? I'm repulsive. I'm absolutely, without a doubt, the most worthless kid on the face of the planet!*

With your head swimming and your stomach full of knots, you curl up in a tiny ball and pray that God will take your life—anything to escape the pain.

Sound familiar? Of course, we all feel down from time to time. But if you've ever experienced this kind of emotional extreme, then you may have had a bout with depression. Each year about one in eight North American teens are diagnosed with this disorder. While the causes are not fully known, depression can affect a person's eating, sleeping, self-perception, and worldview. In serious cases, it can result from a medical condition that requires the help of a therapist.

According to psychologists, depression is more than a passing bad mood that goes away in a couple of days. It's an illness that, if left untreated, can cause physical and emotional damage. It can also ruin relationships, destroy your progress at school or work, and even lead to suicide.

If this is your battle, you're not alone. Above all, understand that you're not weak or somehow un-Christian by admitting you may be depressed. With time, prayer, and treatment, you will feel better. If you think you're depressed, talk to your doctor, minister, or a qualified Christian counselor about what you're thinking and feeling. Turn to the hope and happiness offered in God's Word. He has a positive plan for your life. His Son Jesus values you more than His own life, and He wants your life to be filled with His peace.

Depression will pass, but God's love will remain constant.

WHAT DOES GOD SAY???

God is aware that depression is something common among His people. He knows that we have the tendency to slip into hopelessness, despair, and sadness.

> Without warning, a furious storm came up on the lake, so that the waves swept over the boat. But Jesus was sleeping. The disciples went and woke him, saying, "Lord, save us! We're going to drown!" He replied, "You of little faith, why are you so afraid?" Then he got up and rebuked the winds and the waves, and it was completely calm.
>
> MATTHEW 8:24-26

The Lord's strength is enough to overcome any of life's problems.

> He gives strength to the weary and increases the power of the weak.
>
> ISAIAH 40:29

Even when the world seems to be against you, God is for you.

> "Peace I leave with you; my peace I give you. I do not give to you as the world gives. Do not let your hearts be troubled and do not be afraid."
>
> JOHN 14:27

Hope is a just a prayer away.

> *Why are you downcast, O my soul? Why so*
> *disturbed within me? Put your hope in God, for*
> *I will yet praise him, my Savior and my God.*
>
> PSALM 43:5

HOW DOES THIS AFFECT ME???

Depression is among the most treatable of emotional illnesses; between 80 and 90 percent of people with depression respond positively to treatment. But to begin the healing process, it must first be recognized. Don't ignore the symptoms and give in to a negative and depressing lifestyle. Avoid stimuli, such as music or movies that will only drag you deeper down into a life of despair. Seek out people and messages that will help you look forward to what life has to offer. With God's help, you can put depression behind you.

ANDY JANNING is a True Lies Youth Talks speaker.

Before any of us drew breath, there was a mighty war waging for our souls. This war began with Lucifer, a proud angel of heaven who began to believe in his own power and turned against his loving Creator, God. He thought he could be on equal ground with the Almighty (Isaiah 14; Ezekiel 28) and led a third of the angels into rebellion out of a passion for power. As a result, he and his followers were thrown out of heaven and banished to a place of torture and pain forever—hell. Today we know of them as Satan and demons. They are very real and have only one purpose—to destroy lives. That's right, they want to snag, pull, and trick as many people as possible into their miserable existence.

Not sure you believe in hell? Well, in Jesus' short time on earth, He talked about hell three times more than He did heaven. He warned about this place of torment because He is a jealous God who wants us to spend eternity with Him in heaven. Out of love, He bled and died for us. Through His sacrifice He has opened a path to heaven for any who believe and repent. He has won the battle for us. All we have to do is choose victory.

If you were the devil today, how would you influence people to follow you? First you would start working on people while they're young. How would you send out your message of confusion and deception? You would probably infiltrate their favorite things. You could use everything from music, movies, TV, video games, relationships, and personal life goals. Just slip in little doubts about God and thoughts of self-power. And of course, the haze of alcohol and drugs would help to alter their thoughts and beliefs. Take all things that were created to be beautiful and twist them around. Attack marriage, sex, and family life.

Convince them that purity is silly. Flood them with perversions like pornography and violence. Use all avenues available, including friends, magazines, and even the Internet. Oh yes, most older folks don't even know how to stop them from surfing the Web and checking out whatever they choose. They can bounce from site to site right under their parents' noses. Then, target the very elect. Go for the Christian teens. Neutralize them so that no one will be able to tell them apart from the nonbelievers. Confuse them so that they doubt the true message of Jesus. Keep them busy so that they don't take time to serve God. If you were Satan, you would have to be persistent, because with just one act of obedience to God, these young people could be swept into the protecting arms of God and out of your reach forever.

WHAT DOES GOD SAY???

According to the Bible, we need to know a few things about Satan.
   Read the following verses so you can understand your enemy. Satan lives on the earth. He also isn't the guy in the red suit with horns and a pitchfork.

> How you have fallen from heaven, O morning
> star, son of the dawn!
> You have been cast down to the earth, you who
> once laid low the nations!
>
> ISAIAH 14:12

> The great dragon was hurled down—that ancient
> serpent called the devil, or Satan, who leads
> the whole world astray. He was hurled to the
> earth, and his angels with him.
>
> REVELATION 12:9

> *And no wonder, for Satan himself masquerades as an angel of light.*
>
> 2 CORINTHIANS 11:14

Satan's purpose is to do his best to destroy us and take us to hell with him.

> *Be self-controlled and alert. Your enemy the devil prowls around like a roaring lion looking for someone to devour.*
>
> 1 PETER 5:8

> *"The thief comes only to steal and kill and destroy; I have come that they may have life, and have it to the full."*
>
> JOHN 10:10

Satan's future is to spend eternity in the lake of fire, to be tormented forever.

> *And the devil, who deceived them, was thrown into the lake of burning sulfur, where the beast and the false prophet had been thrown. They will be tormented day and night for ever and ever.*
>
> REVELATION 20:10

We can have victory over our enemy.

> *Submit yourselves, then, to God. Resist the devil, and he will flee from you.*
>
> JAMES 4:7

> *Put on the full armor of God so that you can take your stand against the devil's schemes. For our struggle is not against flesh and*

blood, but against the rulers, against the authorities, against the powers of this dark world and against the spiritual forces of evil in the heavenly realms.

EPHESIANS 6:11-12

HOW DOES THIS AFFECT ME???

The major reason Christians get defeated is that they take the enemy lightly. We must know his ways in order to fight against him, and we must study his weapons and prepare a battle plan. Satan is very smart and powerful, and he knows our weaknesses, too. So take a stand against him daily in the name of the Lord, and you cannot be defeated.

PHIL CHALMERS is the founder of True Lies Youth Talks.

dieting

PHIL CHALMERS

13

I have always loved playing sports. In high school I played football, ran track, and competed in wrestling tournaments. I also spent a lot of time lifting weights. I was young and healthy, and I felt great! All of these activities ushered me right into the tight social circles at my school. My senior year, with a 165-pound body, I was bench-pressing 330 pounds. After graduation I took up bodybuilding and went on to win the Mr. Cleveland bodybuilding contest.

But slowly my life got busier and busier, and I stopped working out altogether. I also started eating whatever I wanted whenever I wanted. The years flew by, and I found myself overweight and unhealthy. I knew what it would take to get back into shape, but I just wasn't motivated enough to make it happen. So I didn't.

I continued to gain more and more weight. By eating the wrong foods and not taking care of my body, I was dying a slow death. At a routine doctor visit, I had my cholesterol checked. I wasn't very surprised to hear that I needed to begin medication to help bring the levels back down to a healthy level. This was my wake-up call. I finally made the decision to take control of my physical body. I stopped letting food control me.

I am in the process of winning, but it is a daily battle. I believe you can win this battle, too. My body is a temple of the Holy Spirit. I'm determined to make it "fit for a king."

WHAT DOES GOD SAY???

Can you imagine being in charge of a temple but not taking care of it? The windows are broken, the shingles are coming off, and the shutters are hanging.

That is the way many of us take care of our temples, our bodies. We can cover our bodies up with baggy clothing, but we can't fool our organs. Many of us will die well before our time due to a poor diet and lack of exercise. Believe it or not, the Bible talks a lot about our physical bodies, diet, and nutrition. Here are a few of those verses:

Your body is the temple of God Himself.

> *Do you not know that your body is a temple of the Holy Spirit, who is in you, whom you have received from God?*
>
> 1 Corinthians 6:19

Don't contaminate your body.

> *Let us purify ourselves from everything that contaminates body and spirit, perfecting holiness out of reverence for God.*
>
> 2 Corinthians 7:1

Our physical body is important to God, but it is not more important than our spiritual well-being.

> *For physical training is of some value, but godliness has value for all things, holding promise for both the present life and the life to come.*
>
> 1 Timothy 4:8

When you doubt whether you can do the next rep or make it to the next healthy meal, remember this verse:

I can do everything through him who gives me strength.

PHILIPPIANS 4:13

HOW DOES THIS AFFECT ME???

The best advice I can give is start today! Follow these five steps to freedom:

1. Cut junk food from your diet: candy, cookies, pies, ice cream, fast food, cheeseburgers, etc. Allow yourself one day a week to cheat, but don't go overboard. Have those foods you've been craving all week.

2. Drink five bottles of spring water every day. Try to drink one bottle with breakfast, one at 10:00 a.m., one at lunch, one at 3:00 p.m., and one with dinner.

3. Start lifting weights and doing aerobic activity three days per week. I lift weights on Monday, Wednesday, and Friday. I do chest and triceps on Monday, legs and shoulders on Wednesday, and back and biceps on Friday. On Tuesday, Thursday, and Saturday, I run for twenty minutes.

4. Eat smaller meals at least five times per day. I eat a healthy breakfast, a protein bar at 10:00 a.m., a healthy lunch at noon, a protein shake at 3:00 p.m., then a healthy dinner. Each meal consists of protein,

carbohydrates, and vegetables. Eat as many fruits and vegetables as you can.

5. If you make a mistake, don't quit. If you cheat, don't give up. Pick yourself up and move forward. If you do the right thing, you will see your body start to change in eight weeks. And in twelve weeks you may start to see that six-pack you have always wanted.

Remember, there are no shortcuts and no magic pills. It's hard work, but you can do it!

PHIL CHALMERS is the founder of True Lies Youth Talks.

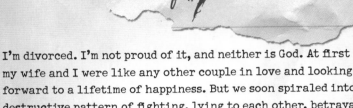

divorce

ANDY JANNING

I'm divorced. I'm not proud of it, and neither is God. At first
my wife and I were like any other couple in love and looking
forward to a lifetime of happiness. But we soon spiraled into a
destructive pattern of fighting, lying to each other, betrayal,
and pain. Two years later our divorce papers stated that we had
"irreconcilable differences." How could we have gone from being
in love to being in court so quickly? We went from signing our
marriage license to suddenly signing our divorce papers. We even
had to sell our wedding rings so we could pay the lawyer's fees.

I'm a Christian, and I know that divorce is a sin. I've heard
it in countless sermons, read about it in the Bible, and learned it
in Sunday school. Unfortunately, we live in a culture that fights
God's principles by offering quick and easy ways out. You've
heard the statistics: More and more couples are walking away
from their commitment to one another. Too many ignore God's plan
for marriage and accept society's lies.

Of course, divorce isn't really easy or painless. Just imagine
throwing away your wedding and honeymoon pictures. Or moving
out of the home you shared to start rebuilding your life—alone.
Or becoming a part-time parent to your kids. Or crying your eyes
out at 3:00 a.m. when you smell your ex-wife's perfume on your
pillow and it finally hits you that she really never is coming
back. Or knowing that you willingly broke your promise to God.
That's right, divorce is neither easy nor painless.

I sincerely hope that you see marriage as a lifelong journey,
not a temporary thrill ride. I pray that you see divorce as the sin
that it is. It is not an easy way out, and it is against God's will
for your life. Love your spouse. Honor your vow. Obey the God who

loves you, and you will find your "happily ever after."

WHAT DOES GOD SAY???

There's no other way to say it: God hates divorce just as He hates all sin.

When you say, "I do," you and your spouse become one. Divorce is ripping that flesh into two.

> *A man will leave his father and mother and be united to his wife, and they will become one flesh.*
>
> GENESIS 2:24

Divorce goes against God's plan for marriage.

> *"Anyone who divorces his wife and marries another woman commits adultery, and the man who marries a divorced woman commits adultery."*
>
> LUKE 16:18

In certain circumstances, though, divorce is permissible. Jesus said that unfaithfulness in marriage and abandonment by an unbelieving spouse make divorce allowable.

> *"But I tell you that anyone who divorces his wife, except for marital unfaithfulness, causes her to become an adulteress, and anyone who marries the divorced woman commits adultery."*
>
> MATTHEW 5:32

*But if the unbeliever leaves, let him do so.
A believing man or woman is not bound in such
circumstances; God has called us to live in
peace.*

1 Corinthians 7:15

HOW DOES THIS AFFECT ME???

Marriage is a preview of heaven (Ephesians 5:22–23). Divorce isn't. Marriage takes love, patience, and sacrifice. Most important, it takes the willingness to forgive as Christ forgives. Just as Jesus forgave the adulterous woman in John 8:1–11, we're called to forgive the sins of a spouse—even if he or she has committed adultery! Resist the sins that can break the bond you have with your spouse. If you're having problems, run to Christ first so you aren't tempted to run away from each other forever.

If you've been divorced, God can forgive you and restore you as a person. He says in 1 John 1:9 that He will forgive your sin and make you a new person. Run to Him, ask for forgiveness, and start your new life in Christ. You might stay single, you might remarry, or God might do a miracle and bring you and your ex-spouse back together again.

Andy Janning is a True Lies Youth Talks speaker.

65

drug use
DANNY HOLLAND

15

"I want to be a drug addict."

Every young person wants to be something when he or she gets older, but I've never heard one express a desire to be a drug addict.

For the past two decades, I have worked closely with thousands of teens. Unfortunately, many were doing drugs. Their reasons vary: "My friends use them," "They make me feel better," "Peer pressure."

Because of my police background, I have a different view of drugs than that of those who are using. I see what their lives will probably look like down the road. I see real-world consequences. I see regrets and pain. I know of students who can never again feel happiness due to permanent brain damage caused by Ecstasy, which they used only once. I have friends who have overdosed on Triple C and nearly died. I know students who were strapped to a table in a mental hospital for a week after taking Oxy. I have never known any person to take drugs who, five years later, thought he or she made a good decision.

Whether you are using drugs or not, I have a question for you: What is your dream? It's a simple question, yet many have not spent the time to think about how to reach their goal. You may not realize it, but God has a purpose for your life. You have been uniquely created by God. You will probably be somebody's future wife, husband, father, or mother. God told Jeremiah something powerful when he was young, and it's true for you today. God told Jeremiah, "I know the plans I have for you. . .plans to prosper you and not to harm you, plans to give you hope and a future" (Jeremiah 29:11). Like Jeremiah, God has an assignment for you that only you can fulfill.

The Bible does not separate drugs from witchcraft. Actually, the Greek word for witchcraft is *pharmacia*, from which we get our word *pharmacy*. They are the same word. When you take drugs, you are actually messing with the enemy—the one whose only purpose is to destroy your life, ruin your future, and rip you off.

Drug use is a sin. It separates you from God, which is the devil's ultimate goal. Jesus came for a different purpose—to give you an awesome life and future.

> *"The thief comes only to steal and kill and destroy; I have come that they may have life, and have it to the full."*
>
> JOHN 10:10

Drugs and alcohol are fun for a while, but they eventually lead to death, which could be physical death, the death of a marriage, or possibly spiritual death.

> *Each one is tempted when, by his own evil desire, he is dragged away and enticed. Then, after desire has conceived, it gives birth to sin; and sin, when it is full-grown, gives birth to death.*
>
> JAMES 1:14-15

You can overcome drugs and resist temptation, but it will take God's help and a very strong will not to give in to Satan's snares.

> *No temptation has seized you except what is common to man. And God is faithful; he will*

not let you be tempted beyond what you can bear. But when you are tempted, he will also provide a way out so that you can stand up under it.

1 CORINTHIANS 10:13

HOW DOES THIS AFFECT ME???

So, how does a drug addiction start? It usually starts by taking drugs that people think they can control, such as cigarettes, alcohol, marijuana, prescription drugs, or over-the-counter medicine. Once Satan has you hooked, he doesn't let up until your life is devastated. The devil has a plan for you—and drugs are just one of his tools to rip off you, your family, and your future family from the benefits of God's plan. If you self-destruct, you will never be able to accomplish God's plan for your life. You will never become the unique person God designed you to be.

God's plan for you is more wonderful than you can imagine. Discover your dream and chase it! The good news is, God forgives! The Bible says, "Anyone, then, who knows the good he ought to do and doesn't do it, sins" (James 4:17). But 1 John 1:9 says that if you confess the sin you know about, God is faithful to forgive you of all unrighteousness. Cool, huh?

Every teen who has decided to take drugs has, at some point, given up on his or her dream. The good news is that God has not given up on His dream for you. You can have a new start today!

DANNY HOLLAND is the True Lies executive director.

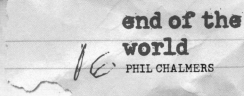

The end times will always be a hot topic. Throughout the years,
many people and religions have predicted the end of the world.
They have given dates and details about when and how it will
happen. But they have all gotten it wrong, because the Bible
clearly states that no one will know the time. Nevertheless, we
can have a better understanding of the events to come by studying
God's Word.

It is very possible that Jesus' return could be this year,
within the next month, or even today. We could surely be living in
the end times right now, for many of the signs the Bible gives us
have been fulfilled. But the one that remains is that every people
and land will hear the message of Jesus Christ. With the daily
devotion of thousands of missionaries, this one last sign may
soon be fulfilled. But even then we will not know the exact time,
because God will come in His own perfect timing—not one minute
sooner or one minute later.

Many believe that a war, sort of like World War III, will
take place in the Middle East. Countries may even deploy nuclear
weapons and destroy large portions of the earth. Once the
Christians are removed from the earth during the rapture of the
church, all hell will break loose.

There will be seven years of chaos called the Tribulation.
Then Jesus will come back and reign on earth for one thousand
years. After that there will be one final battle, and the
Antichrist, Satan, and the False Prophet will be thrown into the
lake of fire. There will be a final judgment for all, and then new
heavens and a new earth will be made. For the rest of eternity,
people will reside in either heaven or hell. If all of this sounds

unbelievable, let's take a look at the Bible verses that describe these events.

WHAT DOES GOD SAY???

Look up the following verses in God's Word that refer to the end times:

- Signs of the end times and Tribulation (Matthew 24:3–31)

- Judgments (Revelation 5–18)

- Seven-year tribulation period (Daniel 9:27; 12:1; Revelation 3:10)

- Second coming of Christ (Matthew 26:64; Acts 1:9–11; Hebrews 9:28; Revelation 1:7)

- Rapture of the church (1 Corinthians 15:50–52; 1 Thessalonians 4:13–18)

- One-thousand-year millennial reign of Christ (Isaiah 11:4–9; Revelation 20:1–3)

- Great White Throne Judgment—for nonbelievers (Revelation 20:12)

- Judgment Seat of Christ—for believers (1 Corinthians 3:10–15; 2 Corinthians 5:10)

- New heavens (Isaiah 65:17; 66:22; 2 Peter 3:13; Revelation 21:1)

- Lake of fire—burning sulfur (Revelation 19:20; 20:10–15, 21:8)

HOW DOES THIS AFFECT ME???

Your view of the end of the world comes directly from where you are in your own spiritual journey. If you are a nonbeliever, your response is probably fear and disbelief. Knowing that your future may include living through the tribulation period is overwhelming. But if you're a believer, your response should be joy and excitement. You can have peace knowing that your place is in heaven and that Jesus is your protector.

It doesn't really matter *when* the Rapture happens as long as you are living your life for Christ. Whether it be in death or during the Rapture, you will be with Christ. First Thessalonians 5:1–3 says, "Now, brothers, about times and dates we do not need to write to you, for you know very well that the day of the Lord will come like a thief in the night. While people are saying, 'Peace and safety,' destruction will come on them suddenly, as labor pains on a pregnant woman, and they will not escape."

Jesus is coming. So be ready. Be ready for judgment. Hebrews 9:27 says, "Man is destined to die once, and after that to face judgment." Two things are guaranteed for most of us. We will die, and we will face judgment. An elect few will be raptured before they face death, but both believers and nonbelievers will face a judgment. Do your best with what you know, and make a difference for Christ. Your reward will be waiting for you in heaven!

PHIL CHALMERS is the founder of True Lies Youth Talks.

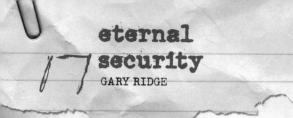

eternal
security
GARY RIDGE

Have you seen the movie _Panic Room_? It's a thriller based on a
mother and daughter pair and their run-in with a pack of thieves.
Their new home is equipped with a state-of-the-art panic room. This
secure room is complete with impenetrable walls, separate phone
lines, ventilation system, and a bank of surveillance monitors
showing most of the home's interior. They run to this room for
protection and security. But as only Hollywood would have it, their
use of this room is their biggest dilemma. The thieves are after
something hidden in that very room. They're trapped. The plot
centers around who will last longer—the intruders or the family
hidden away with no food or water.

Can anything offer total security? Absolutely! God has
invited us to join Him in eternity. Our salvation, through the
saving blood of Jesus Christ, is the only absolute security we can
ever know. It's frightening to ask, "Am I sure I'm going to heaven
when I die? What if Jesus didn't hear me, or what if I didn't say
the right thing when I prayed? What if my sin has caused me to
lose my salvation and now I have to gain it back? How secure am
I after sinning?" Press in toward God. Trust Him with your very
life, and He will give you eternity.

WHAT DOES GOD SAY???

Becoming a Christian is like getting married. I often ask people,
"Are you a Christian?" Sometimes they answer, "I don't know."
Can you imagine asking a married person if he or she is married,
and receiving the reply, "I'm not sure"? Either you _are_ or you
aren't. You know if you have surrendered your life to God. You

also know if you are still
made that commitment to Ch

You can know you have etern

> He who has the Son h
> have the Son of God c
> write these things to
> name of the Son of Go
> that you have eternal

Once you are saved, sealed, and yo ⌐ ⌐ ⌐ ⌐ ⌐ ⌐ ⌐ ⌐ ⌐ook
of life, it will never be erased.

> "I tell you the truth, whoever hears my word
> and believes him who sent me has eternal life
> and will not be condemned; he has crossed over
> from death to life."
>
> JOHN 5:24

> For I am convinced that neither death nor life,
> neither angels nor demons, neither the present
> nor the future, nor any powers, neither height
> nor depth, nor anything else in all creation,
> will be able to separate us from the love of
> God that is in Christ Jesus our Lord.
>
> ROMANS 8:38-39

> And do not grieve the Holy Spirit of God,
> with whom you were sealed for the day of
> redemption.
>
> EPHESIANS 4:30

> "My sheep listen to my voice; I know them, and
> they follow me. I give them eternal life, and

sh; no one can snatch them
Father, who has given them
than all; no one can snatch
Father's hand."

JOHN 10:27-29

ever condemn you once you are a believer in Christ

There is now no condemnation for those who are in Christ Jesus.

ROMANS 8:1

HOW DOES THIS AFFECT ME???

Eternal security gives us the assurance of heaven. It allows us to live this Christian life with peace of mind. But, this does not give us the license to sin. Some believe they can pray a sort of magic prayer, and *poof*, they are saved and can continue in their sin. Others believe Christians can lose their salvation and quote verses like "Work out your salvation with fear and trembling." As Christians we are called to live a Christ-centered life filled with His Holy Spirit. But we are also human, and we will fall from time to time. Jesus understands this better than we do. Ask for forgiveness, and He will always forgive.

So the next time you stumble, review the verses above and rejoice that you are secure in your Father's hand. Know what you believe, and live every day like it's your last.

GARY RIDGE is a True Lies speaker.

fear

JIM BURNS

Enrique was shaking with fear as he stood at the edge of the basketball court. His fellow gang members were lined up in two rows holding bats and clubs, cussing and screaming obscenities at him. Even though he was scared, he knew he had to run the gauntlet. It was the only way out. He was different now, and they wouldn't just let him walk away. This was the pain of leaving the gang. He looked over at Dan, the Christian youth worker who had actually offered to take his place in the gauntlet. He was silently praying for Enrique's life.

Just two weeks earlier, Enrique never would have thought of leaving. But he had gone with Dan and a group of teenagers to a Christian retreat in Wisconsin. He had never been to church before, and he was blown away by God's unconditional love. It didn't matter what he had done, he was loved because he was a child of God. Before the weekend was over, Enrique had become a Christian. He felt great, and everyone seemed to be excited for him—especially Dan.

As they drove closer to Chicago, Dan noticed Enrique was looking very fearful. "What's wrong?" he asked.

"Tonight I have to run the gauntlet," Enrique responded.

"What do you mean?" Dan asked.

"Basically, I'm going to get beat up real bad tonight. When you leave a gang, the members line up in a row with clubs, bats, rings, and their fists. You run down the middle as they give you a beating you'll remember the rest of your life."

Dan asked, "Why tonight?"

Enrique looked at Dan and said, "I can't have Jesus and the gang."

Dan couldn't let him go alone. He walked brave little Enrique to the rundown basketball court where the gang members hung out. Enrique was first to speak. With a shivering voice and fear in his eyes, Enrique told the leader of the gang he needed to run the gauntlet.

"Why? What's wrong?"

His reply was so simple. "I asked Jesus into my heart, and I know I've got to leave the gang."

The leader tried to convince Enrique to give up this Jesus stuff, but Enrique had made up his mind. "Okay, the gauntlet it is," he said.

Dan tried to talk them into not hurting Enrique—but there was no way. Then shockingly, Dan offered to take his place—but it was Enrique's choice and his fate.

Enrique looked at Dan. "Would you really have done that for me?" Dan just put his arm around Enrique and said, "Of course I would."

So there they stood. Dan kept asking, "Is this really happening?"

Enrique looked Dan in the eyes and asked, "Are you absolutely sure Jesus loves me?"

"Yes, He loved you so much He was willing to go to the cross and die for your sins." Dan knew there was a possibility that Enrique was going to his cross for his two-day-old faith in Jesus.

Enrique stepped out in faith and into the gauntlet. He was slugged, hit, beaten, and kicked. Dan begged, screamed, pleaded, threatened, and prayed for the thirteen-year-old life. Enrique was curled up in a ball, trying to protect himself against the blows. At last they called it off. Enrique lay still, bloody and bruised. He couldn't speak or walk. Dan picked up his limp body and carried him twelve blocks to the nearest hospital. They waited three hours for help. Enrique's head was badly cut. His shoulder was enlarged, his groin was swollen to the size of a grapefruit, and he was missing two teeth.

Finally, Enrique was laid on a gurney and taken in for treatment. Dan walked quietly by his side. Enrique looked up at Dan through his bloodshot eyes and bruised face and said, "Jesus really does love me, doesn't He?"

Dan just smiled.

Enrique then added, "He went through extreme pain, even death for me, right?"

Dan nodded.

"Then I'm glad I could go through this for my Savior."

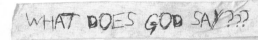

What Does God Say???

God gave Abram and Joshua reasons not to fear.

> The word of the LORD came to Abram in a vision: "Do not be afraid, Abram. I am your shield, your very great reward."
>
> GENESIS 15:1

> "Have I not commanded you? Be strong and courageous. Do not be terrified; do not be discouraged, for the LORD your God will be with you wherever you go."
>
> JOSHUA 1:9

We shouldn't fear people, but instead, fear God alone.

> Fear of man will prove to be a snare, but whoever trusts in the LORD is kept safe.
>
> PROVERBS 29:25

"Do not be afraid of those who kill the body but cannot kill the soul. Rather, be afraid of the One who can destroy both soul and body in hell."

MATTHEW 10:28

HOW DOES THIS AFFECT ME???

Most of the disciples and a lot of early Christians went to their deaths for the sake of the gospel yet didn't fear death. Their faith overcame their fear (Acts 5:17–29). We all want to live without fear. In fact, we admire our heroes because we think they are fearless people who take on and overcome all dangers. The psalmist teaches us that fear of God can lead to a fearless life. To fear God means to respect and revere Him as the almighty Lord. When we do this, we will begin to trust God completely. Only then will our fears subside.

When new situations or surroundings frighten or worry you, recognize that fear is normal. But to be paralyzed by fear is an indication that you question God's ability to take care of you. When we allow our fears to rule our lives, we make them more powerful than God. Recognizing your fear is the first step in committing it to God. Dare to live a life of "No Fear."

JIM BURNS, Ph.D., is the YouthBuilders president.

forgiveness

DOUG HERMAN

Have you ever been betrayed? Have you ever been stabbed in the back with a dagger with the word *saint* inscribed on it? Well I have. It happened in a place and time I least expected. I was a youth pastor of a church in the Denver area and enjoyed spending my life with the sixty teens in the youth group. I also enjoyed coaching wrestling at a nearby high school. One day the senior pastor walked into my office, closed the door, and had a seat. I was completely unaware of the events that were about to unfold. "Doug," he began, "the church board met last night. Your last Sunday is in two weeks."

I was stunned. I asked if I was being dismissed because of a lack of performance or as a disciplinary action or because they perceived I had a moral problem.

"No," he answered.

I then asked if it was because of my wife and daughter's HIV infection—contracted from a blood transfusion.

Again, he said no.

"Then why?" I asked.

"God just told us you need to leave."

Yes, I've removed a dagger from my back. Two years later I found out that it was indeed based on my wife and daughter's infection. Was I angry? You bet. Was I bitter? For a while. And did I ever forgive them? It took time, but yes, I did.

You see, sometimes we experience hurt from others when we are not at fault. "*They* should ask *me* for forgiveness!" I screamed.

But in quiet moments, I could hear Jesus whisper, "I didn't do anything wrong either, and I forgave. Now will

79

you follow My example?"

Forgiving wasn't easy. But it really wasn't for them; it was for me. I was amazed by the freedom I felt. I was released from ugly passion and hatred.

One of the main reasons I can laugh, love, and enjoy life today is because I've learned the power of forgiveness. I forgave the blood donor who lied on his donor form about his sexual past—ultimately infecting my wife and daughter with a deadly disease. And I forgave the church that rejected us when we needed them most. And through it all, God has brought healing.

If you have ever been hurt, and you hold the controls of anger and vengeance, you can find release today by forgiving your offender *first*. It's amazingly freeing—and it's free.

WHAT DOES GOD SAY???

What does it mean to forgive? Webster's online dictionary says it is "to cease to feel resentment against an offender, to grant relief from payment of a debt, to pardon." Everyone has feelings that come and go—and we certainly need to forgive when we feel hurt, but to pardon someone from a debt is powerful! As we meditate on the true meaning of forgiveness, let's look into God's Word and see what the Creator has to say.

What does God say about forgiving those who offend or deeply hurt us?

> *"If you forgive men when they sin against you, your heavenly Father will also forgive you. But if you do not forgive men their sins, your Father will not forgive your sins."*
>
> MATTHEW 6:14-15

> *Bear with each other and forgive whatever*
> *grievances you may have against one another.*
> *Forgive as the Lord forgave you.*
>
> COLOSSIANS 3:13

How can we apply forgiveness from God in areas where we've sinned? And will He forgive?

> *Praise the LORD, O my soul, and forget not all*
> *his benefits—who forgives all your sins and*
> *heals all your diseases.*
>
> PSALM 103:2-3

> *If we claim to be without sin, we deceive*
> *ourselves and the truth is not in us. If we*
> *confess our sins, he is faithful and just and*
> *will forgive us our sins and purify us from*
> *all unrighteousness.*
>
> 1 JOHN 1:8-9

> *"For I will forgive their wickedness and will*
> *remember their sins no more."*
>
> HEBREWS 8:12

HOW DOES THIS AFFECT ME???

Realizing that God will forgive you when you sin is vital. If you didn't know that, today is a wonderful day for you! Regardless of what you've done, God offers you a new start. Ready to begin afresh? Confess your faults, ask for His forgiveness, and enjoy a new life wiped clean by the Creator's compassion.

If you're holding a grudge against someone, today is the day to forgive. It's not easy, but it will do your soul good. When you forgive others, God can forgive you (see Mark 11:25). Go out of your way to meet with your offender and share your forgiveness. The person may receive it or reject it—but doing the right thing will set you free.

Doug Herman is the founder of Pure Revolution. Check out www.PureRevolution.com.

Jana and Krissy lived in the same neighborhood and had been friends for several years. But secretly Krissy was a little jealous of Jana. One day she saw Jana drive off with some older guy after school. She was so curious that she followed them home and watched as they went into Jana's house. Jumping to all kinds of conclusions, she automatically thought that Jana had a new boyfriend. She also speculated about what they were doing all alone inside the house. Soon Krissy had shared her observations with all of their friends. It didn't take long for the rumor to grow wings and fly all over school.

As the story grew, Jana was confronted with all kinds of untrue stories about her. She was shocked when she traced the rumors back to her good friend Krissy. A showdown was inevitable. Jana confronted Krissy, explaining that the older guy was her cousin who was visiting for a few days. Krissy was ashamed, and she was mad at herself for starting such a mess. She asked Jana how she could make it up to her.

After a lot of thought, Jana asked Krissy to lay one piece of paper on the ground at every spot where she had spread the rumor. A little confused, but eager for forgiveness, Krissy did as asked. When she returned, Jana said, "Good, now go back and pick them up."

Krissy looked surprised and exclaimed, "That would be impossible. The pieces of paper will have blown everywhere by now!"

Jana told her that the same was true about her words. As sincere as Krissy was about "making things right," she could never chase down all of her hurtful words.

A gossip betrays a confidence, but a trustworthy man keeps a secret.

PROVERBS 11:13

A perverse man stirs up dissension, and a gossip separates close friends.

PROVERBS 16:28

A gossip betrays a confidence; so avoid a man who talks too much.

PROVERBS 20:19

Do nothing out of selfish ambition or vain conceit, but in humility consider others better than yourselves. Each of you should look not only to your own interests, but also to the interests of others.

PHILIPPIANS 2:3-4

HOW DOES THIS AFFECT ME???

Gossip is never passed along out of compassion. It is, instead, a selfish form of entertainment. It ruins friendships, destroys people's reputations, and is often impossible to take back. But it's so easy to do. We all are guilty of passing along stories when we have no idea if they are true or not. As easy as it may be, it is still unacceptable. Remember, you must treat others as you want to be treated. The next time you think about spreading a story, just imagine if it were a story about you.

ROGER PALMER is a True Lies speaker.

guilt

AARON DAVIS

21

Guilt is very powerful. It is a consuming force that can dominate and consume your mind every second of every day. It stands in the way of peace, real happiness, and growth. It can leave you sleepless and distracted. Shameful memories and thoughts can pierce your heart and soul. But what exactly is guilt? Webster's online dictionary describes it as "the state of one who has committed an offense especially consciously."

I became a Christian in October 1995. Soon after, I found myself in a battle for peace of mind. My mind was plagued with guilt. I couldn't stop thinking about my high school and college days. I had played on the national champion Nebraska football team under coach Tom Osborne, which was a once-in-a-lifetime experience. But I also had bad memories about all the sinful things I had done—lying to young women, misusing alcohol and drugs, cheating, and pretending I was someone I really wasn't just to fit in with the crowd. I had ignored and avoided anything and everything to do with God. Now guilt was robbing me of the joy and peace Jesus Christ wanted for my life.

Jesus died for me out of love. My guilt had gone to the cross with Him—and died. Satan thrives on our past mistakes and tries to hold us captive, but Jesus wants us to be free. The only way to rid yourself of debilitating guilt is to give it to Jesus once and for all. Jesus Christ has already forgiven you, so why not forgive yourself?

WHAT DOES GOD SAY???

If you truly repent, God will forgive your sins and set you free.

As far as the east is from the west, so far has he removed our transgressions from us.

PSALM 103:12

Let us draw near to God with a sincere heart in full assurance of faith, having our hearts sprinkled to cleanse us from a guilty conscience and having our bodies washed with pure water.

HEBREWS 10:22

Then I acknowledged my sin to you and did not cover up my iniquity. I said, "I will confess my transgressions to the LORD"—and you forgavethe guilt of my sin.

PSALM 32:5

There is now no condemnation for those who are in Christ Jesus.

ROMANS 8:1

We have confidence to enter the Most Holy Place by the blood of Jesus. . .having our hearts sprinkled to cleanse us from a guilty conscience and having our bodies washed with pure water.

HEBREWS 10:19, 22

HOW DOES THIS AFFECT ME???

It is not God's plan for us to walk around carrying guilt that He has already forgiven. Stop allowing Satan a stronghold in your life by letting him remind you, over and over, of past mistakes. Go to God, repent, accept His grace, and embrace the freedom of forgiveness.

Reread your Bible. You'll find that many of the main characters, including David, Noah, and Peter, didn't always do things right. Some made very bad decisions that affected the lives of many people for several generations. They committed murder, incest, adultery, and drunkenness. Some even went directly against God and denied knowing Him. But then something wonderful happened: They repented and God forgave them. Many of the great things they did for God came after they were released from their guilt.

If you have done something wrong, you can start by asking for forgiveness. Apologize to whomever you wronged, even if it is yourself. Bow before God and ask for His forgiveness and make a commitment to turn from those actions. Once that is done, move on to the next thing God is calling you to do. Life is too short to live in the past!

AARON DAVIS is a national speaker.

heaven and hell

22 CLINT THOMAS

We have all heard stories of people who died and then came back to life. Some have amazing stories of heaven or hell. Don't you wish they could tell us more? It would be great to hear from someone who has actually experienced either destination. Well, there's good news. Someone has, and his story can be found in Luke 16:19—31. Read it for yourself and discover the story of Lazarus and the rich man.

"There was a rich man who was dressed in purple and fine linen and lived in luxury every day. At his gate was laid a beggar named Lazarus, covered with sores and longing to eat what fell from the rich man's table. Even the dogs came and licked his sores.

"The time came when the beggar died and the angels carried him to Abraham's side. The rich man also died and was buried. In hell, where he was in torment, he looked up and saw Abraham far away, with Lazarus by his side. So he called to him, 'Father Abraham, have pity on me and send Lazarus to dip the tip of his finger in water and cool my tongue, because I am in agony in this fire.'

"But Abraham replied, 'Son, remember that in your lifetime you received your good things, while Lazarus received bad things, but now he is comforted here and you are in agony. And besides all this, between us and you a great chasm has been fixed, so that those who want to go from here to you cannot, nor can anyone cross over from there to us.'

"He answered, 'Then I beg you, father, send Lazarus to my father's house, for I have five brothers. Let him warn them, so that they will not also come to this place of torment.'

"Abraham replied, 'They have Moses and the Prophets; let them listen to them.'

" 'No, father Abraham,' he said, 'but if someone from the dead goes to them, they will repent.'

"He said to him, 'If they do not listen to Moses and the Prophets, they will not be convinced even if someone rises from the dead.' "

From this story we learn that people suffer in hell, they can't leave once they have arrived, and they wish someone could warn their families. And even if they were allowed to come back and tell of the horrors, nobody would believe them anyway. How sad is that?

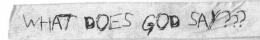

WHAT DOES GOD SAY???

The Bible is clear that when you die, there are only two places to go.

> "They will go away to eternal punishment, but the righteous to eternal life."
>
> MATTHEW 25:46

Heaven is an awesome place. Revelation 21 tells us it is a city with streets of gold, precious stones, no tears, and no death. We will live forever and ever with our Creator, Jesus Christ. Here are a few verses about heaven:

> He will wipe every tear from their eyes. There will be no more death or mourning or crying or pain, for the old order of things has passed away.
>
> REVELATION 21:4

I did not see a temple in the city, because the Lord God Almighty and the Lamb are its temple. The city does not need the sun or the moon to shine on it, for the glory of God gives it light, and the Lamb is its lamp. The nations will walk by its light, and the kings of the earth will bring their splendor into it. On no day will its gates ever be shut, for there will be no night there. The glory and honor of the nations will be brought into it. Nothing impure will ever enter it, nor will anyone who does what is shameful or deceitful, but only those whose names are written in the Lamb's book of life.

REVELATION 21:22-27

Who will go to heaven?

If you confess with your mouth, "Jesus is Lord," and believe in your heart that God raised him from the dead, you will be saved.

ROMANS 10:9

Yet to all who received him, to those who believed in his name, he gave the right to become children of God.

JOHN 1:12

"Not everyone who says to me, 'Lord, Lord,' will enter the kingdom of heaven, but only he who does the will of my Father who is in heaven."

MATTHEW 7:21

What will hell be like?

Then death and Hades were thrown into the lake of fire. The lake of fire is the second death. If

anyone's name was not found written in the book
of life, he was thrown into the lake of fire.

REVELATION 20:14-15

"He who overcomes will inherit all this, and
I will be his God and he will be my son. But
the cowardly, the unbelieving, the vile, the
murderers, the sexually immoral, those who
practice magic arts, the idolaters and all
liars—their place will be in the fiery lake of
burning sulfur. This is the second death."

REVELATION 21:7-8

Who will go to hell?

For. . .God did not spare angels when they
sinned, but sent them to hell, putting them
into gloomy dungeons to be held for judgment.

2 PETER 2:4

And the devil, who deceived them, was thrown
into the lake of burning sulfur, where the beast
and the false prophet had been thrown. They
will be tormented day and night for ever and
ever. . . . Then death and Hades were thrown
into the lake of fire. The lake of fire is the
second death. If anyone's name was not found
written in the book of life, he was thrown
into the lake of fire.

REVELATION 20:10, 14-15

He will punish those who do not know God and
do not obey the gospel of our Lord Jesus. They
will be punished with everlasting destruction
and shut out from the presence of the Lord and
from the majesty of his power.

2 THESSALONIANS 1:8-9

Do you not know that the wicked will not inherit the kingdom of God? Do not be deceived: Neither the sexually immoral nor idolaters nor adulterers nor male prostitutes nor homosexual offenders nor thieves nor the greedy nor drunkards nor slanderers nor swindlers will inherit the kingdom of God.

1 CORINTHIANS 6:9-10

HOW DOES THIS AFFECT ME???

Jesus says in Matthew 7:13, "Enter through the narrow gate. For wide is the gate and broad is the road that leads to destruction, and many enter through it. But small is the gate and narrow the road that leads to life, and only a few find it." Unfortunately, that means that a lot of people are going to hell. That was not God's plan. But through free will, people have the ability to choose for themselves. We are all born into sin, live in sin, and will die in sin if we do not accept salvation through Jesus Christ. It's our choice.

We spend a great deal of time planning our lives. We choose schools, careers, spouses, neighborhoods, and retirement plans. How much time have you spent planning for eternity? It's the ultimate decision with an eternity of consequences. Invest in your future—choose to pursue heaven.

CLINT THOMAS is a True Lies speaker.

I grew up picking rocks, bailing hay, and milking cows on a farm in Pulaski, Wisconsin. It wasn't exactly easy. Yes, we work hard and love our cheese and the Green Bay Packers. We are also proud of our state dance—the polka. We are definitely a different breed of people.

When I was only a few years old, I became addicted to drumming. I'd bang on pots, pans, baking racks, and even Tupperware. After my mom threw out all the dented containers, I discovered other passions to fill my time. I played the piano and sang. During high school, I realized how much I loved to be on stage. I joined mixed choir, vocal jazz, and chamber choir, sang in a barbershop quartet, and performed solos and duets. Shortly after graduation I found that I still had a burning desire to be on stage, but singing soon transformed into my new love—acting.

Realizing the only TV work I could get in Wisconsin was reporting for the Green Bay Packers, I discovered that my newfound love would require a few changes. I packed the back of my rusty '89 Toyota with all of my belongings and headed 2,548 miles west, shouting, "Hollywood, here I come!"

It's working out quite well. I have worked on a lot of movies and TV shows, including *Lizzie McGuire*, *The Young and the Restless*, *Roswell*, *Days of Our Lives*, and *Austin Powers*. I have met and worked with hundreds of famous people, including Geena Davis, Tom Cruise, Heather Locklear, and Kate Hudson.

And I have discovered that Hollywood can be a dangerous place if you don't have a solid relationship with Jesus Christ. I see many young people fall into the trap of drinking, doing drugs, and having sex—a trap that leads to loneliness and confusion. The Hollywood scene is far from glamorous. People are depressed, greedy, and starving for attention. The "big boys" in Hollywood often take advantage of the bright young talent that pours into town every year. They promote the illusion of Hollywood. They tempt with the opportunity of a lifestyle filled with beautiful people and parties. But they neglect to show the consequences of that scene. Don't get caught up in the glamour. Think for yourself and read between the lines. Seek God first, and the rest will just fall into place. Stay grounded, work hard, and think positively.

WHAT DOES GOD SAY???

Most of the messages we get from Hollywood contradict God's will for our lives. Sex, drugs, alcohol, violence, and even suicide are often shown as normal parts of life. Most storylines have main characters who are selfish and will do whatever it takes to get their way. Cheating, lying, and stealing are just means to an end. Does this line up with the message of Jesus? Do these self-centered acts glorify God? How is your everyday life affected by these images and ideas? Check out the following verses.

How are we supposed to react to the messages Hollywood sends?

> *For you were once darkness, but now you are light in the Lord. Live as children of light (for the fruit of the light consists in all goodness, righteousness and truth) and find out what pleases the Lord. Have nothing to do with the fruitless deeds of darkness, but rather expose them. For it is shameful even to mention what the disobedient do in secret.*
>
> EPHESIANS 5:8-12

What's wrong with sex, drugs, and alcohol as entertainment?

Don't you know that you yourselves are God's temple and that God's Spirit lives in you? If anyone destroys God's temple, God will destroy him; for God's temple is sacred, and you are that temple.

1 CORINTHIANS 3:16-17

What's the big deal about people swearing in the movies?

Do not let any unwholesome talk come out of your mouths, but only what is helpful for building others up according to their needs, that it may benefit those who listen.

EPHESIANS 4:29

"Out of the overflow of the heart the mouth speaks. The good man brings good things out of the good stored up in him, and the evil man brings evil things out of the evil stored up in him."

MATTHEW 12:34-35

Out of the same mouth come praise and cursing. My brothers, this should not be.

JAMES 3:10

If this lifestyle is so bad, why is it so popular?

But mark this: There will be terrible times in the last days. People will be lovers of themselves, lovers of money, boastful, proud, abusive, disobedient to their parents, ungrateful, unholy, without love, unforgiving, slanderous, without self-control, brutal,

not lovers of the good, treacherous, rash,
conceited, lovers of pleasure rather than
lovers of God—having a form of godliness but
denying its power. Have nothing to do with
them.

2 Timothy 3:1-5

HOW DOES THIS AFFECT ME???

Be aware of what you watch and what you listen to. If you want a happy, healthy God-filled lifestyle, you need to refrain from anything that goes against God's Word. I am commonly asked, **"Is an *actor* a *real person*? Is what he/she does on screen really who they are?"**

My answer is *yes*! How people act on screen and in the movies is what they believe and what they promote. If they aren't acting out what they truly believe, then they are hypocrites. When you see Jason Biggs having sex before marriage in *American Pie II* and hear Juliet Lewis talking about having a threesome in *Old School*, they believe what they are doing is right.

Beware of the movie rating system. For example, PG-13 shows are really R-rated movies with just enough trimmed to make them PG-13. Go to www.screenit.com and www.pluggedinmagazine.com for a review of a movie before you see it. These Web sites will not only help you make wise decisions, but they will also help you to avoid supporting the wrong movies financially. Why spend your hard-earned dollars supporting garbage that goes against God, His Word, and what you really believe? Stay positive and do your best, and God will be pleased!

Tina Marie Holewinski is a True Lies speaker.

homosexuality

LONNY HARPER

24

Luke is a good kid. He has great parents who are prominent leaders in their local church. They attend church several times a week as a family. He knows everyone, and they all love him. He is always friendly and kind to everyone he comes across. But it's just a mask. Every time he steps out of his room, he hides behind that great big smile. Inside, he is full of shame and confusion. He's tired of playing the game, but he doesn't know what else to do.

He's scared to say the words, "I'm gay." But he lives in a whirlwind of questions and fear. He knows what the Bible says, but everyone else says it's okay. He wonders, *Was I born this way? Will my parents hate me? Will God help me? Will they let me come back to church? Why me?* He wants to confess, but he's terrified of rejection. The contradiction between God's Word and the world's message fuels the fire of confusion.

Do you relate to Luke's anguish? If not, then maybe some of your friends do. Sin in our lives, even sin hidden behind a mask, will be revealed sooner or later. Take charge of your life. Confess, cry out to God, and let the healing begin.

WHAT DOES GOD SAY???

Yes, homosexuality is a sin, and everyone is born with a sinful nature. Every Christian is engaged in a battle either to be led by God's Spirit, who is in us, or led by our flesh (sinful nature). Therefore, Christians struggling with homosexuality are engaged in a battle between the Spirit and their flesh. But Jesus died on the cross for *all* sinners. This includes murderers, thieves, liars, adulterers, and homosexuals. We are commanded to love others as Christ loves us. If you know people who struggle with homosexuality, pray for them and share the love of Jesus with them. Don't mock or attack them. Love them into an abundant life in Christ. After all, that's what Jesus did for us.

Is homosexuality wrong?

> Therefore God gave them over in the sinful desires of their hearts to sexual impurity for the degrading of their bodies with one another. They exchanged the truth of God for a lie. . . . Because of this, God gave them over to shameful lusts. Even their women exchanged natural relations for unnatural ones. In the same way the men also abandoned natural relations with women and were inflamed with lust for one another. Men committed indecent acts with other men, and received in themselves the due penalty for their perversion. . . . Although they know God's righteous decree that those who do such things deserve death, they not only continue to do these very things but also approve of those who practice them.
>
> ROMANS 1:24-26, 32

> "If a man lies with a man as one lies with a woman, both of them have done what is detestable."
>
> LEVITICUS 20:13

> Do you not know that the wicked will not inherit the kingdom of God? Do not be deceived: Neither the sexually immoral nor idolaters nor adulterers nor male prostitutes nor homosexual offenders nor thieves nor

the greedy nor drunkards nor slanderers nor
swindlers will inherit the kingdom of God.

1 CORINTHIANS 6:9-10

What if I struggle with homosexuality?

God demonstrates his own love for us in this:
While we were still sinners, Christ died for us.

ROMANS 5:8

Flee from sexual immorality. All other sins
a man commits are outside his body, but he
who sins sexually sins against his own body.
Do you not know that your body is a temple of
the Holy Spirit, who is in you, whom you have
received from God? You are not your own; you
were bought at a price. Therefore honor God
with your body.

1 CORINTHIANS 6:18-20

How should I treat someone who struggles with homosexuality?

Dear friends, let us love one another, for
love comes from God. Everyone who loves has
been born of God and knows God.

1 JOHN 4:7

Jesus replied: " 'Love the Lord your God with
all your heart and with all your soul and with
all your mind.' This is the first and greatest
commandment. And the second is like it: 'Love
your neighbor as yourself.' "

MATTHEW 22:37-39

"Do not judge, or you too will be judged. For in the same way you judge others, you will be judged, and with the measure you use, it will be measured to you."

MATTHEW 7:1-2

When they kept on questioning him, he straightened up and said to them, "If any one of you is without sin, let him be the first to throw a stone at her." . . .Those who heard began to go away one at a time, the older ones first, until only Jesus was left, with the woman still standing there. Jesus straightened up and asked her, "Woman, where are they? Has no one condemned you?" "No one, sir," she said. "Then neither do I condemn you," Jesus declared. "Go now and leave your life of sin."

JOHN 8:7, 9-11

HOW DOES THIS AFFECT ME???

If you struggle with homosexuality, there are no easy answers. It can bring you into bondage just like any other sin. Please understand that God offers forgiveness upon confession of your sin. First Corinthians 6:9–10, quoted above, begins by naming those who will not be going to heaven, including homosexual offenders, and then the next verse says, "And that is what some of you were. But you were washed, you were sanctified, you were justified in the name of the Lord Jesus Christ and by the Spirit of our God" (1 Corinthians 6:11).

If a friend is facing this challenge, be sure to demonstrate God's love while speaking the truth. It's easy to walk away—but that doesn't show God's love. There are many resources to help people through this struggle. Check out Focus on the Family's Web site, www.family.org, for materials. If you are struggling with homosexuality, you don't have to figure this out all by yourself. There are people who care and are ready to walk you through this time in your life. And remember, God loves you right now, just as you are.

LONNY HARPER is a national speaker.

humility

MATT PELISHEK

25

The evening started out great. I headed out into a cold North Dakota night to watch my friend Alissa play volleyball. The game was fun, and Alissa played well, as usual. But I was more excited about our date after the match. It was just going to be a quick bite to eat, but I was really looking forward to it. While Alissa was getting ready, I ran out to start my van. Our winters were like a deep freeze inside of an igloo. As I walked her out, I realized that I had locked my doors. My keys were in the ignition, the car was running, and all of my doors were locked. I couldn't believe it.

We jumped into Alissa's car and ran around town, looking for help. Finally, we retrieved a tool that opens locked car doors. As we drove back to my van, I was determined to fix this problem with plenty of time left for the date, even though I had never used one of these tools before. But I'm a guy. I'm supposed to know how to use tools, so I was sure I could figure it out. I got busy turning, pulling, and pushing the tool around. Twenty minutes later, the van was still locked and my hands were freezing. But I wasn't going to give up.

Finally, Alissa asked if she could give it a try. *Sure*, I thought, *if I can't get it, there's no way she'll be able to*. Within sixty seconds, I heard a *click, pop, creak!* I turned around to see Alissa standing there beside the open door. I was so embarrassed. If only I had asked for help instead of trying to be the hero, we would have already been on our date.

I gained a little humility that day. It's a simple, yet effective, story. When I think I can do it on my own, God always finds a way to set me straight. Let's take a look at what the Bible says about humility and its counterpart, pride.

Lessons in humility always come at the worst times. But would we remember them if they didn't? The Bible is full of such lessons. Read Daniel 1; Exodus 3 and 4; and Numbers 12:3.

What do we gain from humility?

> Humility and the fear of the LORD bring wealth and honor and life.
>
> PROVERBS 22:4

> "If my people, who are called by my name, will humble themselves and pray and seek my face and turn from their wicked ways, then will I hear from heaven and will forgive their sin and will heal their land."
>
> 2 CHRONICLES 7:14

Can we be hurt by choosing to be proud and not humble?

> "God opposes the proud but gives grace to the humble."
>
> JAMES 4:6

> Pride goes before destruction, a haughty spirit before a fall. Better to be lowly in spirit and among the oppressed than to share plunder with the proud.
>
> PROVERBS 16:18-19

> "For everyone who exalts himself will be humbled, and he who humbles himself will be exalted."
>
> LUKE 18:14

The founder of True Lies, Phil Chalmers, says jokingly, "I'm humble and proud of it." It's funny but often true. Many of us are proud of our "humble" actions. But humility and pride are opposites: We can't be both humble and proud at the same time.

Martin Luther said, "God created the world out of nothing, and as long as we are nothing, He can make something out of us."

French dramatist Ernest Legouve said, "If he could only see how small a vacancy his death would leave, the proud man would think less of the place he occupies in his lifetime."

The Bible says that pride comes before a fall. If we choose pride, we will be humbled. If we humble ourselves, then God will pour out His blessings into our lives.

MATT PELISHEK is a True Lies speaker.

As Christians we are to live a life that points to Christ and His love. But reality comes along and reminds us that we aren't perfect yet. What are we supposed to do with these embarrassing moments? How often do we make decisions or comments that are contrary to our belief? We may move along not even realizing that we have left a lasting, and negative, impression on others. It's overwhelming to realize that we are Christ's representatives here on earth. People are watching—and they will uncover a fake every time. If we serve Christ with honesty and humility, His love will shine through—even when we mess up. But if we wear a Christian mask, we will surely be found out.

I learned this lesson early. As a young Christian, I had the opportunity to attend an out-of-state weekend of worship with my church. To save on expenses, I was asked to ride along with an older couple. Marge and Bill seemed like such a happy, friendly pair. They always had a smile and a warm "Hello" when they greeted people in the chapel on Sundays. And they were quick to share what God was doing in their lives and to praise Him.

But the trip quickly became very interesting. I was shocked when Bill began to make racist remarks and tasteless jokes about the people we passed on the road. He even teased that he could "earn points" for each person he could run over! My jaw dropped and my stomach sickened as this "godly" couple openly laughed at those who were different from them.

How could Bill be the same person whom I had heard talk about the love of God? How could Marge sing praise songs to God and laugh at her husband's gross behavior? During that seemingly endless drive, I racked my brain trying to make sense of it all, but I couldn't. Did they really not see their own hypocrisy? All I could do was pray that God would keep me from being as blind to my wrongdoing as Bill and Marge were to theirs.

WHAT DOES GOD SAY???

Hypocrisy is about being inconsistent. Hypocrites may appear to be living for God, but their hearts are polluted by sin, which they are either unable or unwilling to see. Jesus used strong words against the hypocritical religious people of His day. He warned His followers not to get caught up in a similar "show" of religion by seeking attention for their offerings, their prayers, or their fasting (Matthew 6:2, 5, 16). Our goal should not just be to look good on the outside, but to allow God to mold us into His image, inside and out.

How can we fail to see our own sin?

> "Why do you look at the speck of sawdust in your brother's eye and pay no attention to the plank in your own eye? How can you say to your brother, 'Let me take the speck out of your eye,' when all the time there is a plank in your own eye? You hypocrite, first take the plank out of your own eye, and then you will see clearly to remove the speck from your brother's eye."

MATTHEW 7:3-5

How can we avoid hypocrisy and be consistent?

> Do not merely listen to the word, and so deceive yourselves. Do what it says. Anyone who listens to the word but does not do what it says is like a man who looks at his face in a

mirror and, after looking at himself, goes away and immediately forgets what he looks like. But the man who looks intently into the perfect law that gives freedom, and continues to do this, not forgetting what he has heard, but doing it—he will be blessed in what he does.

JAMES 1:22-25

They claim to know God, but by their actions they deny him. They are detestable, disobedient and unfit for doing anything good.

TITUS 1:16

How do we respond to hypocrites?

Let us fix our eyes on Jesus, the author and perfecter of our faith.

HEBREWS 12:2

Brothers, if someone is caught in a sin, you who are spiritual should restore him gently. But watch yourself, or you also may be tempted.

GALATIANS 6:1

HOW DOES THIS AFFECT ME???

It's so easy to be blind to our own sin. It's much easier to ignore it than it is to deal with it. But God wants us to be holy—and *wholly* His. In Matthew 23 Jesus called the religious people of the day hypocrites at least six times in one chapter. If you want to know the definition of a hypocrite, read Jesus' example in Matthew 23. My favorite part is Matthew 23:27, where Jesus says, "You are like whitewashed tombs, which look beautiful on the outside, but on the inside are full of dead men's bones."

If you have a secret sin, take care of it today. Get help and pray that God will let you know when pride, hate, envy, or secret sins creep into your life. He can help you handle hypocrisy. He can also help you avoid getting tripped up when you see others fail to live up to His standards. Remember to follow Him, not them. God can always be trusted to lead you in the right direction. Now go and do the right thing!

CAPTAIN CHRISSY ROCK is the children's ministry outreach director for the Salvation Army, USA East.

One of my favorite television programs is *Sports Center* on ESPN. Not many people who are crazy about sports pass up the opportunity to kick back on the couch with a bag of chips and a Coke to watch ESPN's amazing coverage of everything from football to Chinese Ping-Pong. Each week I look forward to the regularly scheduled segment of *Sports Center* titled "Sunday Conversation." During this segment, the viewers are privileged to hear from some of the world's greatest athletes on topics ranging from sports to family life and faith.

One conversation in particular really stood out for me. Warren Sapp, defensive stud for the world champion Tampa Bay Buccaneers, took on some tough questions one Sunday morning. Sapp responded eloquently to a question about fans who like to criticize the way he plays the game. "I think it's great that so many fans show up to these games and root us on. Fans help to make the game of football as popular as what it is; however, it bothers me when people come to these games, sit in the stands, eat junk food, and then make comments about how I could have done a better job. Until these people get up and get on the gridiron, down here on the battlefield where the game is played, I ignore them. Unless you've played this game at the level in which we play, you have no idea what it takes."

Without realizing it, Warren Sapp accurately described a lot of Christians. Too many sit back, observing the world around them, only to formulate opinions about how the world *should be.* Our world is full of Christians who line the pews on Sunday mornings shouting "Amen!" when the preacher talks about the need for love in the world. These same people walk out of the church *talking* about how great the message was but don't do anything to change the world. Only a few actually move past the *talking* stage into the *action* stage. The majority are just spiritually lazy.

Jesus Christ calls His followers to overcome spiritual laziness, which can lead to arrogance, pride, gossip, and more. He is calling His followers to put down the junk food, get out of the stands, get into the game, and be the followers He called them to be. There is a difference between being a *Christian* and being a *Christ-follower*. Many people call themselves Christians, but they aren't truly following Jesus. True followers of Jesus overcome spiritual laziness by standing up to make a difference in their world. Are you spiritually lazy? Will you overcome your complacency? What's your game plan?

WHAT DOES GOD SAY???

When we think about laziness, we form pictures in our mind of an out-of-shape person lying on the couch with greasy hair, dirty sweat pants, and potato chip crumbs and French onion dip stains on his T-shirt. He's watching old reruns of the *Dukes of Hazzard*, *COPS*, and *Jerry Springer*. Certainly, a person who fits this description may be lazy, but laziness is much more than this stereotypical image formed in your mind. Many lazy people are judgmental and think they know it all yet refuse to get involved to better a situation. Laziness can overpower the unlikeliest person without him or her even realizing it. The Bible warns us to avoid laziness for good reasons.

> *The sluggard's craving will be the death of him,*
> *because his hands refuse to work.*
>
> PROVERBS 21:25

> *We do not want you to become lazy, but to*
> *imitate those who through faith and patience*
> *inherit what has been promised.*
>
> HEBREWS 6:12

Here Jesus is talking about laziness and offering advice on how to handle lazy workers.

> "His master replied, 'You wicked, lazy
> servant! So you knew that I harvest where
> I have not sown and gather where I have not
> scattered seed? Well then, you should have put
> my money on deposit with the bankers, so that
> when I returned I would have received it back
> with interest. Take the talent from him and
> give it to the one who has the ten talents. For
> everyone who has will be given more, and he will
> have abundance. Whoever does not have, even what
> he has will be taken from him. And throw that
> worthless servant outside, into the darkness,
> where there will be weeping and gnashing of
> teeth.' "
>
> MATTHEW 25:26-30

Instead of being lazy, discover your gifts and make a difference in this world.

> Each man has his own gift from God; one has
> this gift, another has that.
>
> 1 CORINTHIANS 7:7

Out of love for others, step out and help them see what life is really about, and guide them to Jesus Christ, the author of life.

> "My command is this: Love each other as I have
> loved you. Greater love has no one than this,
> that he lay down his life for his friends."
>
> JOHN 15:12-13

HOW DOES THIS AFFECT ME???

People who are spiritually lazy are people who don't understand their ministry or what God has called them to do. Will you get in the game or will you be one of those people who Warren Sapp was referring to when he was interviewed on ESPN? Will you be a person who does nothing more than observe, criticize, judge, and act like you know it all? Or will you become a player in the game of life? Overcoming spiritual laziness is a process—so get started today. Time is short, and the people around you are searching for the answers. It's time to make a difference!

JIM GRAY is a Student Ministries pastor and True Lies speaker.

Recently I was a guest on the *Howard Stern Show*. I debated the violent band Insane Clown Posse. They brag about killing women, cutting people's throats, stabbing, and using hatchets. I did my best to stay focused on the lyrics of this band and how they market and sell violence and obscenity. I thought the debate went pretty well considering we were on the *Howard Stern Show*.

I was amused that Stern and the band didn't want me in the studio for the interview. They said I would make the band feel uncomfortable. I thought that was kind of strange since this band's music is so violent.

This type of contradiction is not uncommon. Many artists live one way but promote a totally different lifestyle in their music, videos, books, or Web sites. Eminem raps about being a role model, saying, "Smoke weed, take pills, drop outta school, kill people, and drink." But in real life he doesn't imitate his message. He doesn't let his own daughter listen to his music, nor does he swear around her. He wakes up in the morning and eats cereal with her, watches *Power Puff Girls*, plays Barbie dolls, and drives her to school. The same mother he kills in his songs, he lived with until he was twenty-six. Most bands will promote anything that will bring in big money. But does that make it okay? I don't think so, because the things being promoted affect people, especially children.

In an early song from Jay-Z, he mentions a certain brand of vodka—it flew off the shelves across the country. So he and his label, Roc-a-fella Records, decided to make their own brand of vodka just so they could market it in their songs. They actually own their own distillery. The same goes for clothes, shoes, and whatever else the artists are singing or rapping about. As consumers we must realize that we are affected by these images. We need to increase our own awareness of the messages we take in on a daily basis. Once we're aware, it is a lot easier to discern between the good and the bad.

Many people think music, movies, and video games are nothing more than entertainment. Think again! The Bible has a lot to say about what we listen to, watch, and look at.

WHAT DOES GOD SAY???

We need to renew our minds and fill them with things that are pure and holy.

> Do not conform any longer to the pattern of this world, but be transformed by the renewing of your mind. Then you will be able to test and approve what God's will is—his good, pleasing and perfect will.
>
> ROMANS 12:2

> Finally, brothers, whatever is true, whatever is noble, whatever is right, whatever is pure, whatever is lovely, whatever is admirable—if anything is excellent or praiseworthy—think about such things.
>
> PHILIPPIANS 4:8

Sin is a progression. It starts out with just a crude song or a game but can lead to death—both physical and spiritual—if we are not careful.

> But each one is tempted when, by his own evil desire, he is dragged away and enticed. Then, after desire has conceived, it gives birth to

sin; and sin, when it is full-grown, gives birth to death.

JAMES 1:14-15

Music was created by God for His worship. Your music should direct your thoughts to God.

Speak to one another with psalms, hymns and spiritual songs. Sing and make music in your heart to the Lord.

EPHESIANS 5:19

Last, we need to take control of our thoughts.

We take captive every thought to make it obedient to Christ.

2 CORINTHIANS 10:5

HOW DOES THIS AFFECT ME???

Challenge yourself by asking, "Do I support entertainment that goes against God's principles?" If the answer is yes, you need to find new entertainment (Ephesians 5:1–15). Realize that you are a role model. Younger siblings, friends, and family members are watching. Luke 17:1–3 talks about the consequences of making God's children stumble. Above all, strive for a life of holiness. Stay connected to God, let Him lead you, and avoid all types of evil (Psalm 101). If something isn't drawing you closer to Christ, then stop wasting your time and energy. The choice is yours—do the right thing!

PHIL CHALMERS is the founder of True Lies Youth Talks.

When I felt the Lord leading me into the ministry, I prayed, "God, I don't want to be just another preacher. There are lots of preachers—on the radio, TV, doing this, doing that—they're everywhere." God spoke to my heart and said, "Well, don't be *just* another preacher."

I realized that if Christians are going to change the world, we must expand our sight and catch a glimpse of God's vision. It's one that reaches to the ends of the earth. In scripture, God's heart for the world is complete. Revelation 14:6 records John's vision of an angel who will carry God's message in the end times: "He had the eternal gospel to proclaim to those who live on the earth—to every nation, tribe, language and people." This passion is God's distinct mark of love in our lives. The first thing people should notice about us is our unashamed desire for God.

As a world changer, you must allow the bigness of God's vision to influence your own. You have to think globally, look at the big picture, and sense God's heart. It doesn't matter if you live on a foreign mission field or in small town America. But it does make a difference whether you have allowed God to guide your life in a way that points to Him and His vision.

Meditate and chew on this principle all day long. God's heart for every tongue, tribe, and nation is an essential part of what makes Him tick. We are often distracted by all of the busyness in life—our activities, sports, fun, and games. God is thinking about the end of the earth and the tribes that never had a chance. Let His heart for the whole world begin to color your vision. Think, pray, live, and inspire bigger.

Live on the edge. Get radical for Jesus. Pursue a life that will turn people's hearts toward God. Whether you minister in this nation or overseas, your ministry will prosper if you lay your life on the line for Christ. God wants us to have the passion and determination to live for Him—on the edge!

WHAT DOES GOD SAY???

Why should I go on missions?

"Therefore go and make disciples of all nations, baptizing them in the name of the Father and of the Son and of the Holy Spirit."
MATTHEW 28:19

*"I took you from the ends of the earth, from its farthest corners I called you.
I said, 'You are my servant'; I have chosen you and have not rejected you."*
ISAIAH 41:9

After this I looked and there before me was a great multitude that no one could count, from every nation, tribe, people and language, standing before the throne and in front of the Lamb. They were wearing white robes and were holding palm branches in their hands.
REVELATION 7:9

Where do I start?

You affect the people closest to you, such as your family and friends, but you may feel called to fulfill your ministry as an apostle, prophet, evangelist, pastor, or teacher (Ephesians 4:11)—to go out into the world. Begin by ministering where you are right now. I hear young people say, "Well, I would witness to my friends, but I really feel called to Russia." God may have called you overseas, but right now He has planted you at your school, in your community, and with your friends for a reason. Prove yourself faithful today so God can send you out tomorrow.

> But in your hearts set apart Christ as Lord. Always be prepared to give an answer to everyone who asks you to give the reason for the hope that you have. But do this with gentleness and respect.
>
> 1 PETER 3:15

> Live such good lives among the pagans that, though they accuse you of doing wrong, they may see your good deeds and glorify God on the day he visits us.
>
> 1 PETER 2:12

HOW DOES THIS AFFECT ME???

Ministry has no age limit. Young, old, and everyone in between are invited to share the Good News. God will use you if you are willing. He is not looking for someone with great talent or someone who has the Bible memorized. He is looking for someone just like you—someone willing to change the world by obeying His Word and His Spirit.

More and more teenagers are going on mission trips each year. They say, "I'm tired of my world revolving around me. I want to favor others, give myself away, and be selfless for the gospel of Jesus Christ. I want to see lives drastically changed." Is that what you're thinking? Have you gotten started?

Have the vision of a world changer. Be full of God's vision by seeing the big picture. Get a glimpse of what God is doing, and do everything you can to be a part of it. Start now—change the world!

RON LUCE is the founder of Teen Mania. Have questions? Want to learn more about Teen Mania's mission trips? Log on to www.TeenMania.org.

modesty

NANCY ALLEN

Here's a message for all of the young ladies out there—it *does* matter what you wear. Like most girls, you probably like to dress trendy. You love to wear today's hottest styles. But have you noticed a shift in today's clothing trends? Shirts are tighter, shorter, lower-cut, and backless. Some T-shirts are small enough to fit your little sister! Some even have sexual messages on them. Jeans are dangerously low. Skirts and shorts are teeny-tiny. Dressing sexy is definitely in.

So what's the big deal? Well, unfortunately, today's styles reinforce a stereotype women have been fighting for centuries. It's one that bases our worth on our bra size instead of our brain size! Young female pop artists aren't making it any easier. They start the trends, and everyone scrambles to keep up. But every time a girl buys and wears skimpy clothes, she reinforces the stereotype. You may say, "What's wrong with dressing a little 'flirty'? So what if I flaunt my hot little body? It's empowering, because it gets a guy's attention, right?" It sure does, but that doesn't make it right.

Here's the deal. Dressing sexy is not honoring to God. If you're a Christian, you represent Christ, and your job is to draw others to Jesus. If you choose to wear sexy clothes, you will instead draw attention to yourself. You will send the message, "I am interested in being pursued sexually." Even if you have chosen to be sexually abstinent, dressing provocatively sends a very different message. You come across as a hypocrite. Every time you bare your navel, your integrity as a Christian is compromised.

Dressing sexy also causes your brothers in Christ to stumble.

A girl in tight clothes is a stumbling block for guys. Jesus tells us in Matthew 5:28 that lust is a sin. And since guys are weak in the area of visual stimulation, you are causing them to lust. You are helping them to sin. Have you ever thought about that? If you could get into a guy's head for just a few minutes, you'd get it. Visual temptation is really tough for them. So ask yourself, "Am I dressing to honor God? Am I helping or hurting those around me?"

WHAT DOES GOD SAY???

Your beauty should not come from outward adornment, such as braided hair and the wearing of gold jewelry and fine clothes. Instead, it should be that of your inner self, the unfading beauty of a gentle and quiet spirit, which is of great worth in God's sight.

1 PETER 3:3-4

But among you there must not be even a hint of sexual immorality, or of any kind of impurity, or of greed, because these are improper for God's holy people.

EPHESIANS 5:3

Do not cause anyone to stumble.

1 CORINTHIANS 10:32

I also want women to dress modestly, with decency and propriety, not with braided hair or gold or pearls or expensive clothes, but with good deeds, appropriate for women who profess to worship God.

1 TIMOTHY 2:9-10

HOW DOES THIS AFFECT ME???

Think about all of the cheap cars out there. There are a lot of economy cars, pickups, SUVs, new and used, trying to get your attention. Commercials, signs, billboards, and radio ads announce the latest and greatest deal. Why? Because they need all of the extra stuff to get any attention. Now think about how many ads you have seen for expensive cars. Have you ever come across a commercial for a Rolls Royce? I didn't think so. Why—because they are the real deal. If you're in the market for a high-end car, you know what you want and where to get it. Advertising isn't really necessary.

So ladies, are you an old pickup or a Rolls Royce? Class and character—not showing off your belly button—will attract the right kind of guys.

Modesty means manifesting humility (being humble, not drawing attention to yourself), propriety (what's proper, righteous, correct behavior), and restraint (the act of holding back, showing limitations, and *self-control*). Self-control is one of the fruits of the Holy Spirit!

By dressing modestly, you may be passed over a few times for the girl who dresses like a little hottie. It's really okay to be overlooked by a guy who's only interested in your body. Dressing respectably will attract someone who likes you for who you are on the inside and out. I'm not saying that you need to start dressing like a grandma. Just make wiser choices. If you feel that some of your clothing might be questionable, just don't wear it. Allow the Holy Spirit to guide you. You are a child of God, so let Jesus shine through you. He is your true beauty!

NANCY ALLEN is a True Lies speaker.

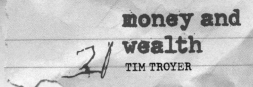

money and wealth

TIM TROYER

Taggu leaned on his hoe and squinted up at the field as the afternoon sun beat down on his tired shoulders. Finishing the hot, dusty job would take two more full days of work. Then they would move on to the next field. Ramesh, his nine-year-old son, brushed the sweat from his eyes and hoed the scrubby weeds around him. Even though he worked hard, Taggu worried about him. He was small for his age and didn't get much to eat. It hurt to see the other village boys on their way to school while Ramesh worked with him in the fields from sunup to sundown. Slave life sure wasn't easy, especially in southwestern Nepal.

It's hard to believe that slavery still exists in the world, but it does. In many countries, people like Taggu and his family live in a crushing cycle of poverty, without hope of escape. Our lives are so different than theirs.

Taggu wasn't always a slave. Before I met him, he was a carpenter in a small village. One day his wife got very sick and had to be rushed to the doctor. Nepal, one of the poorest countries in the world, doesn't have enough doctors, and the medicine is very expensive. Taggu's wife was diagnosed with leprosy and needed a large volume of medicine over the course of a year to get well. Taggu sold all of his tools to buy the medicine. When the medicine ran out, he sold himself into slavery to buy more. When it ran out the second time, his master offered to buy his son Ramesh for eight hundred dollars. With no place left to turn, he was faced with the agonizing life-and-death choice between his wife's life and his son's freedom. He chose life.

Wealth is what separates developed countries such as the United States from poor, underdeveloped countries like Nepal.

123

Wealth is simply the ability to produce more than you need to survive. You may not think of yourself as rich, but you probably are compared to many people in the world. We are blessed. And we are also accountable for how we choose to use our riches. We are not only supposed to take care of ourselves, but to help those around us as well. Wealth is not just money—it's freedom. It means safety, food, shelter, and clothing. So you don't feel rich? Take some time to imagine a day in the life of Ramesh.

Working with other Christians, my friends and I were able to raise enough money to help Taggu and his family. We bought them, and a little over a hundred families, out of slavery. We just gave from the heart. One teen from my church gave her birthday money—it was all she had. In American standards, it wasn't much. But that small amount was enough to buy one man out of slavery. He is free today because a young girl cared enough to share what God had given to her. It doesn't take much to make a difference!

WHAT DOES GOD SAY???

The Bible talks a lot about wealth. It warns about trusting in riches and being greedy, but it also tells us that God rewards obedience with blessings. The key is to look at giving from God's perspective and purpose.

Where does true wealth come from?

> But remember the LORD your God, for it is he who gives you the ability to produce wealth.
>
> DEUTERONOMY 8:18

> Every good and perfect gift is from above, coming down from the Father of the heavenly lights, who does not change like shifting shadows.
>
> JAMES 1:17

Isn't money the root of all evil? No, but the love of money is.

> *The love of money is a root of all kinds of evil. Some people, eager for money, have wandered from the faith and pierced themselves with many griefs.*
>
> 1 TIMOTHY 6:10

> *Of this you can be sure: No immoral, impure or greedy person—such a man is an idolater—has any inheritance in the kingdom of Christ and of God.*
>
> EPHESIANS 5:5

What does God want us to do with wealth?

> *Always give thanks to God the Father for everything, in the name of our Lord Jesus Christ.*
>
> EPHESIANS 5:20

> *Religion that God our Father accepts as pure and faultless is this: to look after orphans and widows in their distress and to keep oneself from being polluted by the world.*
>
> JAMES 1:27

> *Command those who are rich in this present world not to be arrogant nor to put their hope in wealth, which is so uncertain, but to put their hope in God, who richly provides us with everything for our enjoyment.*
>
> 1 TIMOTHY 6:17

HOW DOES THIS AFFECT ME???

Christians in the United States spend more money feeding their pets than they do feeding starving people. They also spend more on soft drinks and snack food than they do on spreading the good news of Christ. What a shame. God has blessed us so that we can help others, not so we can hoard it all. It's a sin to be selfish and greedy. Taggu and Ramesh are free today because ordinary people shared what they had. I pray that God will help you to know true wealth. Invest in others and support ministries that are making a difference in the world.

Take time right now to thank God for freedom, food, shelter, and clothing. Next time you are tempted to complain—*don't!* Be thankful. Make it your goal to have ownership of things, but don't let things own you. Take inventory. What do you have to share? If you don't plan to be generous, it won't happen. Send a gift to a ministry that needs your help to reach out to people who are hurting spiritually or physically. It will change your life and the lives of others!

TIM TROYER is the pastor of Berlin Christian Fellowship.

murder

JAMIE ROUSE

I'm a murderer. You might think it takes a horrible person to commit murder. That isn't true. I was just an average kid with the same dreams as everyone else. But when I got to high school, things began to change. One of my friends introduced me to heavy metal music. I constantly listened to bands like Pantera, Saigon Kick, and Alice in Chains. Soon I began to believe the messages of anger and hopelessness. As my attitude grew darker, so did my music. I even got into bands that glamorized violence and murder. I had rejected God, which opened the door for all kinds of evil. So the thought of murder didn't seem so horrible. I began to listen to death metal bands like Obituary, Napalm Death, and Morbid Angel. The music made me feel capable of murder, which felt like a rush of power. I would also watch all kinds of horror movies. They made murder look so easy, so glorious.

As problems grew in my life, so did my anger and hopelessness. I got to the point where I just wanted it all to end. I wanted to die. I blamed others for my misery even though it was my own fault. I left for school one day, expecting not to come back alive. But at the end of the day, I found myself in a jail cell. I could hear a television in the background reporting what I had done. I broke down and cried. I cannot describe the pain I felt. The movies and the music never said anything about this part of murder. The pain afterward is something that I will never fully recover from.

Some music and movies glorify murder. They're written and produced by people who have never killed. Unfortunately, they don't tell the whole story. But I can tell you from experience that it's horrible. No one should take the life of another human.

127

Movies and music didn't make me do it, but they did give me a false impression about killing someone. Ultimately, it was my choice—a choice made out of ignorance and stupidity. Because of what I did, families were shattered, and I will never get out of prison alive. In some aspects, my life ended that day—standing in a school hallway with a gun in my hand. I shot three people, killing two. I'm now a murderer. And I'm only seventeen years old!

WHAT DOES GOD SAY???

In God's eyes, hating others is just as bad as murder.

> *"You have heard that it was said to the people long ago, 'Do not murder, and anyone who murders will be subject to judgment.' But I tell you that anyone who is angry with his brother will be subject to judgment."*
>
> MATTHEW 5:21-22

> *Anyone who hates his brother is a murderer, and you know that no murderer has eternal life in him.*
>
> 1 JOHN 3:15

One of the Ten Commandments prohibits murder.

> *"You shall not murder."*
>
> EXODUS 20:13

Murder starts in the heart.

> *"Out of the heart come evil thoughts, murder, adultery, sexual immorality, theft, false testimony, slander."*
>
> MATTHEW 15:19

HOW DOES THIS AFFECT ME???

As a result of our fallen nature, everyone is capable of murder. That's not a pretty thought. You may think you would never take someone's life. But when I started high school, I never thought in a million years I would kill someone either. No one is immune.

The Bible says that whoever hates his brother is a murderer. That's a disturbing thought. As long as you hold on to hate, you're viewed the same as Timothy McVeigh or Jeffrey Dahmer in the eyes of God. So be quick to get rid of hate and swift to forgive.

If you hear of someone who may be plotting murder, take that person seriously. Try to help that person deal with his or her problems in a nonviolent way. If the person won't listen, call the police. He or she may get arrested but will thank you in the end.

Some signs to look for in a desperate person who may be plotting murder are violent outbursts, slipping grades, change in behavior, and stress. Even if the person is not considering murder, he or she still needs help. It's better to be safe than sorry. And remember, we need to be careful of what kind of music we listen to and what kind of movies we watch. First Corinthians 15:33 says, "Bad company corrupts good character." Even to the point of murder!

JAMIE ROUSE was involved in a school shooting at Richland High School in Tennessee. Have questions? Contact him at this address: Jamie Rouse, #284025, SCCC, Box 279, Clifton, TN 38425.

parents

PHIL CHALMERS

22

I didn't grow up on the *Leave It to Beaver* TV show. Nor did I grow up in Mayberry on the *Andy Griffith Show*. I wish I had. I didn't even grow up in a Christian family. And I never attended a youth camp, youth conference, overnighter, or weekend retreat as a teenager. How sad is that?

Many teens complain about their parents, and sometimes they may have reason to complain. But instead of looking for the bad in your parents, why not look for the good? The fact that you have one or two parents is a blessing. Many people have no parents, are in foster homes, or are locked up in prison. My friend, rapper LG Wise, has never met his dad, and his mom gave him away when he was little. Whatever your situation is, you have to feel blessed if you have at least one parent in your life.

Most of you have parents who love you, and if they are Christians, that is an extra bonus. If they care enough about you to encourage you to go to church, you are fortunate. You will thank them many years down the road. I wasn't extremely close to my dad, and even today we don't speak much. He's had a hard life and has a hard time communicating with me. I understand that, and I love him anyway. My mom and I are pretty close, but she had a rough upbringing as well and has made mistakes along the way. I guess what I am saying is, if you are looking for perfect parents, like on *Leave It to Beaver*, dream on! That's not reality. Your parents will make mistakes, so move on—forgive them, love them, and cherish them.

Even though we know parents will make mistakes, God commands us to obey and honor them. At a minimum, loving them might allow God to convict them for their wrongdoing, abusive talk, hateful behavior, or mistakes. It may even save their soul. The only time this doesn't apply is when your parents are committing crimes or physically or sexually abusing you. If this happens, you need to tell someone you trust, such as a pastor, youth leader, teacher, or police officer.

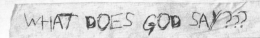

WHAT DOES GOD SAY???

Obey your parents.

> *Children, obey your parents in the Lord, for this is right.*
>
> EPHESIANS 6:1

> *Children, obey your parents in everything, for this pleases the Lord.*
>
> COLOSSIANS 3:20

Honor your parents.

> *Honor your father and your mother, so that you may live long in the land the LORD your God is giving you.*
>
> EXODUS 20:12

> *"Honor your father and mother"—which is the first commandment with a promise—"that it may go well with you and that you may enjoy long life on the earth."*
>
> EPHESIANS 6:2-3

Not honoring and respecting your parents brings consequences.

> *If a man curses his father or mother, his lamp will be snuffed out in pitch darkness.*
>
> PROVERBS 20:20

HOW DOES THIS AFFECT ME???

You will never understand how tough it is to be a parent until you are one—especially in the world we live in today. I thought I was a youth expert until my wife and I adopted our eight-year-old boy six years ago. From that day forward, I realized that parenting wasn't going to be easy. It's very challenging, and there are many decisions to make. And yes, you who are reading this will make lots of mistakes when you are a parent, and your kids will notice as well!

Love your parents. Understand that they care about you and that it is their job to take care of you and to guide you, protect you, and steer you in the right direction. Stop fighting them and start respecting them. Obey them. Honor them. By putting this advice into practice, you will find that you will get along with them. And when that happens, trust begins. With trust comes freedom, and you will finally have the trust and space you always wanted by doing it the right way—God's way!

PHIL CHALMERS is the founder of True Lies Youth Talks.

As a youth pastor, I look back on my years as a teenager and see peer pressure from a whole new perspective. I became a Christian in 1994 during the summer break following my sophomore year. Prior to that commitment to Christ, peer pressure had ruled my life. I remember a time, right after I got my driver's license, when I was driving and one of my good friends drove up beside me and asked me if I wanted to race all the way out to his house. Now, you know that if I backed out of this challenge, he would have rubbed it in my face and called me a chicken, and he probably would have told everyone else that I was scared. Without a thought, I said, "Let's go!"

As we were racing, the lead changed hands quite a bit. We were passing each other on two-lane roads at incredible rates of speed. We came up on the last turn that approached his neighborhood, and I decided that this was my last chance to take the lead, so I floored it. As I started to pass him, my car went too far over to the left and I began to slide on gravel and lost complete control of my car. My car ended up crossing lanes directly in front of his car, barely missing it, and crashed head on at eighty-five miles per hour into an embankment. My car flipped several times, and I was ejected from the vehicle. I barely escaped death as the car ran over my leg, and when it was over, I was laying in the ditch.

The police came, and an ambulance took me to the hospital. Luckily, I didn't suffer any permanent injuries. I had to pay for court costs and fines, and my car was totaled. Following this incident, I reflected back on the many times that I said I would never race or drive at excessive speeds. I couldn't believe I had done this; I was so embarrassed. It seemed like something just came over me. Well, that something was peer pressure. I remember the times when my friends and I would be together and one of them would say suggest stealing something to see if we could get away with it, or another would say, "Let's try smoking marijuana; it can't be that bad." Why is it that we will do things with our friends that we typically wouldn't do alone? The reason is peer pressure. Why do you think peer pressure is so intense? Let's see what the Bible says.

WHAT DOES GOD SAY???

When talking about peer pressure, you need to ask yourself a couple of questions: "Have I let others pressure me into making bad decisions? Are certain friends and/or activities pulling me away from God? Do I influence others, or do they influence me?"

> My son, if sinners entice you, do not give into them. If they say, "Come along with us; let's lie in wait for someone's blood, let's waylay some harmless soul. . .throw in your lot with us, and we will share a common purse" —my son, do not go along with them, do not set foot on their paths; for their feet rush into sin, they are swift to shed blood. . . . These men lie in wait for their own blood; they waylay only themselves!
>
> PROVERBS 1:10-11, 14-16, 18

> Do not be misled: "Bad company corrupts good character."
>
> 1 CORINTHIANS 15:33

"You are the light of the world. A city on a hill cannot be hidden. Neither do people light a lamp and put it under a bowl. Instead they put it on its stand, and it gives light to everyone in the house. In the same way, let your light shine before men, that they may see your good deeds and praise your Father in heaven."

MATTHEW 5:14-16

He who leads the upright along an evil path will fall into his own trap, but the blameless will receive a good inheritance.

PROVERBS 28:10

HOW DOES THIS AFFECT ME???

Peer pressure doesn't have to affect you at all. You have a choice in the matter; you have the ability to change the outcome of what peer pressure is intended for. Can one person really affect a whole group? Is it possible to steer your peers in the right direction when they're going the wrong way? Yes!

To not be influenced by peer pressure, set some standards now. Be firm in what you believe, with no hesitation. Let people know that although you like them, you can't do certain activities. Why? Because you don't believe in those sorts of things. Be loving but firm. If they know you're serious, they will respect you, and you will then start to influence them.

Stop giving in to peer pressure today and start living as a child of God and a light to this world. Stand up for what you believe in and say no to the things that go against godly principles. If you do this, God will honor you for obeying His

Word. Seek His face, read His Word, and be like the house built on the rock. When the winds blew, it was not shaken.

JASON ROSE is a youth leader with Berlin Christian Fellowship.

pornography and lust

BRIAN
a fifteen-year-old-student

It's hard to believe, but five years ago (when I was only ten) I helped to produce an illegal pornographic Web site—one that featured underaged models. My story could fill the pages of an entire book, so I won't go into all the details. Instead, here's how I'll sum up my actions: I'm ashamed.

I wish I could erase the images that haunt me every day. I wish I could change history and regain my innocence. I can't. But I know that I'm forgiven through Jesus Christ, my Savior. Through Him I have a new life and a future filled with hope. And that's what I'm going to share with you today—the greatest decision I've ever made!

It happened one winter during church camp. I guess more than anything else I just wanted to get away from my unhealthy situation, even if only for a weekend. My plan was to have a good time and not think about the mess I'd made of my life, but I guess God had other plans for me those few days. He clearly laid on my heart that I needed to give up what I was doing and let Him take the reins of the situation. I wrestled with God over the reality of my situation: I was involved in producing an illegal pornographic Web site that used minors, and my boss would try to hurt me if I quit. Yet God wanted me to trust that He would take care of me if I would give my situation to Him.

On the last night, I took the first step and told my best friend everything that was going on. He supported me and encouraged me to speak with the youth pastor. He then advised me to do three things: pray, tell my parents, and pray some more to seek out God's will.

That afternoon when I got home, I told my parents

127

everything. Fortunately, they weren't mad at me, but they were concerned for obvious reasons. We called my uncle, who is a police officer, and he came up with a plan. With six plain-clothed police officers stationed around my home, I called the man I had been working for and informed him of my immediate resignation. He said, "Don't go anywhere, I'm coming over."

Within an hour the man pulled up in front of my house and got out of his car with three of his skinhead friends. He rang the bell, and I opened the door only to explain to him again that I couldn't do it anymore, that my relationship with God was more important. He quickly reached behind him as if to pull something out when my uncle came out from behind me along with the two officers waiting in my entryway. They told him as well as the other three that they were under arrest for hosting illegal Web sites with underage porn, for employment of minors, for possession of weapons, and for carrying illegal drugs. The man I worked for was promptly prosecuted and sentenced to a seven-year jail term in a state penitentiary.

Doing the right thing can be difficult at times, especially when it means opening yourself up to others and exposing your sin to them without knowing how they will respond. For me, the battle for my sexual purity is not over; it has just begun. I know I will continually have to battle the images that are in my head, which came through the industry I promoted by poorly using the gifts God gave me.

WHAT DOES GOD SAY???

Read what Jesus thought about pornography and lust.

> "You have heard that it was said, 'Do not commit adultery.' But I tell you that anyone who looks at a woman lustfully has already committed adultery with her in his heart. If

*your right eye causes you to sin, gouge it
out and throw it away. It is better for you
to lose one part of your body than for your
whole body to be thrown into hell."*

MATTHEW 5:27-29

Read how Paul describes the struggle of sin versus godly living.

*I do not understand what I do. For what I want
to do I do not do, but what I hate I do. And
if I do what I do not want to do, I agree that
the law is good. As it is, it is no longer I
myself who do it, but it is sin living in me.
I know that nothing good lives in me, that is,
in my sinful nature. For I have the desire to
do what is good, but I cannot carry it out.
For what I do is not the good I want to do;
no, the evil I do not want to do—this I keep
on doing. Now if I do what I do not want to
do, it is no longer I who do it, but it is sin
living in me that does it. So I find this law
at work: When I want to do good, evil is right
there with me. For in my inner being I delight
in God's law; but I see another law at work
in the members of my body, waging war against
the law of my mind and making me a prisoner of
the law of sin at work within my members. What
a wretched man I am! Who will rescue me from
this body of death? Thanks be to God—through
Jesus Christ our Lord!*

ROMANS 7:15-25

**All sin left unconfessed becomes addictive and will eventually
take the place of God controlling our thoughts and actions. It
will also become our place of refuge or our escape in times of
trouble.**

Do not let sin reign in your mortal body so that you obey its evil desires.

ROMANS 6:12

HOW DOES THIS AFFECT ME???

Both guys and gals are looking at porn. And if you are not looking yourself, you probably have a friend—maybe a boyfriend or girlfriend—who is. Porn is an epidemic that touches many people. Since it only takes three to five days to get addicted to porn, we need to stay away from it, treat it like a drug, and have zero tolerance. We need to guard our eyes and make sure we are not lusting after the opposite sex. We also need to make sure we are not causing people to sin by the way we dress, act, talk, or carry ourselves.

If you are already addicted to porn, here are three steps to take. First, confess it to God. He has said in 1 John 1:9 that He wants to forgive you, but the first step is confession. Next, and this is the hardest, confess it to someone else. Since porn is a dirty little secret, most people tell no one. Tell a friend, relative, or youth leader (see James 5:16). And third, take practical steps to keep from going back. Put your computer in the living room and only go online when someone is present. Use the software from XXXchurch.com that e-mails a friend who can hold you accountable if you fail at avoiding these sites. Take this one day at a time, and you can keep your mind and thoughts pure.

CRAIG GROSS and TROY BUSHER cowrote this lesson.
Both are on staff at XXXchurch.com.
(Additional contribution by Gary Ridge,
True Lies national speaker.)

pregnancy

SARA GRIVAS

I remember the moment I learned that I was pregnant. A mix of emotions raced through me—everything from joy to fear. A precious young life was growing inside of me!

At the same time, I felt very overwhelmed. This wasn't the right time or the right way. I wasn't even married. What was I supposed to do? There was no easy answer. I was faced with a decision that would affect the rest of my life. How did I get to this point? Why me?

I was very successful in high school. I entered college pursuing an engineering degree. School was great, and I was in love and ready to rule the world! I was dating my high school sweetheart, and we were planning to get married after graduation. Not being Christians, we didn't think having sex was that big of a deal. We were in love!

But there I was—pregnant. Just six months before the end of my junior year. I had spent a lot of time planning the most amazing fairy-tale wedding and honeymoon. Suddenly I just felt young and scared. But I knew that abortion was not an option. It just didn't seem right. After all, having a baby couldn't be that hard. (My mom had seven!)

Well, I did get a wedding. Even though it was beautiful, it wasn't even close to my dreams. We threw things together quickly so we could have the ceremony before I began to *look* pregnant. We took the only available date left—April Fool's Day. My parents were so unhappy and embarrassed. And we didn't run off on a beautiful Caribbean trip. No, we went ice fishing up north. I had robbed myself of the wedding and honeymoon of my dreams.

Even though we moved in with my brother, we still weren't able to make it on my husband's income. I worked as a waitress for a while just to pay the bills. I was ready to return to school when I got the news that I was pregnant again. It had only been seven months! I didn't get to graduate with all of my friends. They moved on to big jobs, traveling, and nice cars. Meanwhile, my world was crumbling. Our marriage slowly deteriorated and eventually ended in divorce. I left the marriage in pursuit of a "happier life." Before long I was pregnant for the third time. There I was with two kids, divorced and pregnant. I was miserable. But I was determined to finish my degree. And I just couldn't bear facing my parents again. So I turned to a different solution— abortion. I thought that I could get rid of my little "problem" and move on with my life.

Years later I was in love again and planning another wedding. Before that glorious day, I became pregnant again for the fourth time. I was devastated as I dropped out of school— again. I decided to stay home and raise this child myself. My two older children hadn't done so well after being shoved into daycare while I selfishly pursued my own goals.

Looking back, I could have made better choices. First, I could have chosen the best form of birth control—abstinence. Second, I could have given my third child the chance for a wonderful life through adoption. Instead, I continued to push for my own selfish ambitions and desires. I never put my kids first. They experienced an angry atmosphere, an unhappy mom, and the devastation of divorce. And one didn't even have a chance at that. From the very first moment that I became sexually active, I had always put myself first. I was all about me! And my kids have had to pay the price.

Trust in the LORD with all your heart and lean not on your own understanding; in all your ways acknowledge him, and he will make your paths straight.

PROVERBS 3:5-6

"For I know the plans I have for you," declares the LORD, "plans to prosper you and not to harm you, plans to give you hope and a future."

JEREMIAH 29:11

"Listen to me, O house of Jacob, all you who remain of the house of Israel, you whom I have upheld since you were conceived, and have carried since your birth.
Even to your old age and gray hairs I am he, I am he who will sustain you. I have made you and I will carry you; I will sustain you and I will rescue you."

ISAIAH 46:3-4

I praise you because I am fearfully and wonderfully made; your works are wonderful, I know that full well.
My frame was not hidden from you when I was made in the secret place.
When I was woven together in the depths of the earth, your eyes saw my unformed body.
All the days ordained for me were written in your book before one of them came to be.

PSALM 139:14-16

HOW DOES THIS AFFECT ME???

When it comes to pregnancy, you always have choices. If you or your friend is pregnant, check out all of the options. Turn to someone you trust. Find a Christian adult who can offer you guidance and prayer during your pregnancy. You also have to tell your parents. It will be hard, but it is absolutely necessary. Stepping up and taking responsibility is best for everyone involved.

If you're a teenager, seriously consider adoption. Many married couples are praying for a baby. They wait patiently for the opportunity to care for and love a child of their own. It is a selfless act that will allow your child to grow up in a loving home with both a mother and father. It is truly the least selfish thing you could do for your child. If you want to raise the child on your own, talk to other single moms first. Even though they love their children, they will be the first to let you know how hard it is. Just ask yourself, "What is the best choice for my child?"

You must also understand that abortion does not get rid of the "problem." The pain and shame will stay with you forever. God will forgive, but you will have to live with the reality that you chose death for your own child.

If you're trying to help a friend out, remember that you cannot make this decision for her. Be a good friend and pray for her daily. Remember that we are all human and we make mistakes. Lead her to seek God's will above all else. With His forgiveness and guidance, she will have the strength to make the best choice for her child. God will use her (your) situation for good some-day—trust me!

SARA GRIVAS is a True Lies speaker.

These last few years have been really good for Pillar. We've won three Dove Awards and had a handful of number one radio singles and good record sales. To top it all off, we just signed a mainstream record deal with MCA Records. When we play live shows, people hold up huge signs that say, PILLAR ROCKS. Fans make homemade T-shirts that say, PILLAR RULES. Sometimes there are even a bunch of girls up front yelling, "We love you." After our shows we head off to the autograph table where hundreds of fans line up just to say hi and get our autographs.

Now you're probably asking yourself, "How in the world do these Christian guys keep their pride in check?" The only way to overcome something as strong as pride is through prayer and realizing that it's not all about Pillar. We ask God to help keep us humble and work through us. Remembering to thank God for all He has done is a very important part of staying humble. Great things happen because of God's blessings—not our own actions.

WHAT DOES GOD SAY???

Having pride is sinful.

> *Haughty eyes and a proud heart, the lamp of the wicked, are sin!*
>
> PROVERBS 21:4

God will humble and punish the proud.

*"God opposes the proud
but gives grace to the humble."*

JAMES 4:6

*The LORD detests all the proud of heart. Be
sure of this: They will not go unpunished.*

PROVERBS 16:5

*Pride goes before destruction, a haughty
spirit before a fall.*

PROVERBS 16:18

We should hate pride and instead choose to be humble.

*"I, wisdom, dwell together with prudence; I
possess knowledge and discretion.
To fear the LORD is to hate evil; I hate pride
and arrogance, evil behavior and perverse
speech."*

PROVERBS 8:12-13

HOW DOES THIS AFFECT ME???

Is pride really that great a sin? If you made a list of sins (such
as murder, rape, pride, and adultery), pride wouldn't seem so bad.
Wrong! Just reading the verses above clearly shows how much God
despises it. When we have a prideful attitude, we are basically
telling God, "Hey, I can do this my way; look at what I've done so
far." And when we try and do things our way, it's hard for God to
work in our lives and bless us.

God has a much better plan for our lives than we can even

imagine. Drop the pride and let God have control. Things will happen much faster and better that way. Start today by realizing that all you do is through God. All of your accomplishments are actually gifts He has given you. It's exciting to know that God has chosen to give you unique and special gifts to use in this life.

KALEL is the bass player for Pillar.
To get more info on the rock band Pillar, log on to www.PillarMusic.com.

prison
LG WISE

28

Bang, bang, bang! It was 6:00 a.m. in Mod 6, Cellblock C74, of Riker's Island Prison Camp, New York, New York. "Get up everybody! It's time for count, and if anybody wants breakfast, move it now!" The correctional officer's billy stick bounced off the metal bars as he walked along. This was the guy who would be telling me when to eat, shower, sleep, work, walk, and even go to the bathroom for the next twenty-five years to life. What did he mean "wake up"? It's not like I got much sleep. I was too busy watching my back. There were thugs, murderers, and criminals everywhere. I figured I was one of them now. That's what I got for not cooperating with the Feds. Welcome to hell!

Before long I had a court date. A shot at freedom! I didn't know what to expect. I was transported to the courtroom, chained to twenty other criminals in the back of a hot police truck. I cried out to God, "If You get me out of this mess, I promise I'll go where You want me to go. I'll do what You want me to do. I'll say what You want me to say." I couldn't help but wonder, *Can God hear someone like me?* As I stood in front of the judge, I was blown away when he said, "I grant this young man time served. You're free to go." Those words were music to my ears. The judge granted me time served! God must have heard me! He had mercy!

Today I'm trying to keep my promise to God. I'm now a Christian rap artist sharing God's message of hope and salvation. God heard my prayer then—and He is still listening today.

God cares about those in captivity or prison. He also urges us believers to reach out to those in prison, to visit them and care for them.

He has sent me to bind up the brokenhearted, to proclaim freedom for the captives and release from darkness for the prisoners.

ISAIAH 61:1

"The LORD looked down from his sanctuary on high, from heaven he viewed the earth, to hear the groans of the prisoners and release those condemned to death."

PSALM 102:19-20

Remember those in prison as if you were their fellow prisoners, and those who are mistreated as if you yourselves were suffering.

HEBREWS 13:3

"Then he will say to those on his left, 'Depart from me, you who are cursed, into the eternal fire prepared for the devil and his angels. For I was hungry and you gave me nothing to eat, I was thirsty and you gave me nothing to drink, I was a stranger and you did not invite me in, I needed clothes and you did not clothe me, I was sick and in prison and you did not look after me.' "They also will answer, 'Lord, when did we see you hungry or thirsty or a stranger or needing clothes or sick or in prison, and did not help you?' "He will reply, 'I tell you the truth, whatever you did not do for one of the least of these, you did not do for me.' "

MATTHEW 25:41-45

149

God looked down from heaven, heard my cry, and opened the doors. I was guilty, and He offered me freedom. If you know someone who has walked away from God, pray for his or her reunion with our Creator. If the person is actually in prison, you can share the many stories of the New Testament. Many were unjustly locked up because of their beliefs and faith. Even Jesus was arrested, detained, and executed. He knows exactly what they are going through. And Christ offers every person freedom, even if he or she is behind steel bars. Praise God!

LG WISE is a rap artist.

purity

TRICIA BROCK

When I was fourteen, the teens in my youth group decided to make a "True Love Waits" pact. I remember it like it was just yesterday. I stood in front of my church and promised to remain pure. My parents bought me a pendant that symbolized my decision before God, family, friends, and myself. The pendant had three question marks that represented the questions I could ask when tempted: *How is this decision I am about to make going to affect God? How is it going to affect others in my life? How will it affect me?* I remember wondering, *Can a little pendant around my neck really keep me in check?* It sure did. Not because it was magic or good luck, but because it was a reminder about what I believe.

Like most teens, I was starting to face big decisions at a young age. I felt pressure to let go of some of my innocence, go along with the crowd, and be cool. I even struggled with whether I was going to date or not. At times I felt very alone. It seemed that all of my friends were dating cute boys, becoming popular, and having a lot of fun. They seemed to feel really good about themselves. Before long I watched as they were disappointed and hurt and eventually fell away from God. I knew that I had to decide what was more important. Would I choose my relationship with God or my social status? I chose God. I wanted to be the kind of woman Proverbs 31 talks about. I wanted my beauty to come from the inside, from fearing and loving God.

High school got a little tougher, but with God's strength, I made it through. He became my best friend, and I learned what it meant to pray without ceasing. I began to walk in the Spirit every day, not leaving God at home or in my prayer closet.

As I look back at the past twenty-three years of my life, I realize what purity has meant to me. It's not a line I drew or some religious rule. It's a sacrifice and choice I made to honor God. I remain pure because of my love for God. Even though I sin and make mistakes sometimes, I know that I must press on. And I will never forget that God looks at the heart, and I want my heart to be beautiful to Him!

WHAT DOES GOD SAY???

Some teens have a hard time with the word *purity*. It means much more than just being sexually pure (although that's vital!). It's about pure passion, honor, leadership, and strength. Having a pure heart is the key to a pure connection with our Creator. And our relationships with others should reflect our purity, too (see Proverbs 31; 1 Corinthians 6:18–20; and 1 Thessalonians 4:3–7).

How would you define *purity*? (Hint: pure sugar, pure gold, or pure heart.)

> *We know that when [Christ] appears, we shall be like him, for we shall see him as he is. Everyone who has this hope in him purifies himself, just as he is pure.*
>
> 1 JOHN 3:2-3

> *Create in me a pure heart, O God, and renew a steadfast spirit within me.*
>
> PSALM 51:10

> *Charm is deceptive, and beauty is fleeting; but a woman who fears the LORD is to be praised.*
>
> PROVERBS 31:30

Why is purity important in our lives?

"Blessed are the pure in heart, for they will see God."

MATTHEW 5:8

Marriage should be honored by all, and the marriage bed kept pure, for God will judge the adulterer and all the sexually immoral.

HEBREWS 13:4

If you're not perfect, can you become pure today?

The blood of Jesus, [God's] Son, purifies us from all sin.

1 JOHN 1:7

If we confess our sins, he is faithful and just and will forgive us our sins and purify us from all unrighteousness.

1 JOHN 1:9

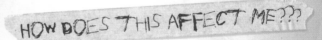

HOW DOES THIS AFFECT ME???

One of my favorite scripture passages is Job 23:8–12:

"But if I go to the east, he is not there; if I go to the west, I do not find him.
When he is at work in the north, I do not see him; when he turns to the south, I catch no glimpse of him. But he knows the way that I take; when he has tested me, I will come forth as gold. My feet have closely followed his steps; I have kept to his way without turning aside.

*I have not departed from the commands of his
lips; I have treasured the words of his mouth
more than my daily bread.*

I challenge you to make the right choice. Wake up and choose to live for God—not yourself. That has been my heart's desire since I was fourteen years old. And after all the testing, trials, and struggles that life brings my way, God knows me. He sees me and my heart. His plans for me are good, and I want to come out of the fire as pure gold. To be beautiful in His eyes is the only kind of beauty that will last forever!

*Written by TRICIA BROCK, lead vocalist, Superchic[k].
Scripture help from Doug Herman, founder of Pure
Revolution, www.PureRevolution.com.*

rape

REBECCA JONES

40

He was athletic, good-looking, polite, smart, and quite a gentleman. These are just a few of the amazing qualities that attracted me to Jake. I wasn't alone; every girl at school thought he was great. He charmed his way into everyone's heart. I was no exception. The summer after my junior year, Jake was actually pursuing me! Our first date was dinner at a cute little Greek restaurant followed by a romantic walk downtown. I was hooked. This guy was everything I dreamed of. I waited anxiously as days went by without my hearing from him.

He just showed up one night as I walked to my car. I was surprised but happy. He said he had a special night planned and talked me into going with him. I knew I had to be home early, and he promised he would have me home in time. We made various stops at bars as we walked downtown. My discomfort level rose as Jake became increasingly drunk. He kept trying to get me to drink, and I kept reminding him that I wasn't twenty-one yet.

As we finally headed to the car, I insisted he drive me straight home. He drove right past my house and chuckled as he said, "Just you wait." I thought to myself, *Whatever kind of surprise you have planned, I'm just not interested.*

About a mile past my house is a deserted area next to a lake. He parked his truck off the road and turned off the headlights. He was prepared. He had blankets and pillows all ready for "stargazing." But instead, I became a victim of date rape. He began to forcefully kiss me so I couldn't talk. He held my hands down and used his legs to separate mine. My cold body froze as he said things like, "If you would just relax, this would be a whole lot easier."

I clearly remember the potent smell of alcohol on his breath as he verbally and sexually abused my lifeless and unresponsive body. He passed out a few hours later. I carefully searched for my clothes and ran back to my house. I headed straight for the bathroom. As I showered, the scalding hot water burned my skin. I wanted to destroy any memory of what had happened to me that night. By being infatuated with the man of my dreams and letting my guard down, I became a victim of rape.

WHAT DOES GOD SAY???

God speaks very clearly on His stance against rape (Deuteronomy 22:28–29). He is grieved when His children (young or old) endure pain and become innocent victims of violent crimes. But through His power, we can overcome. Here are some verses God wrote specifically to people who have suffered because of crimes such as rape.

What does God want to do with us after something horrible happens?

> *"For I know the plans I have for you,"*
> *declares the LORD, "plans to prosper you and*
> *not to harm you, plans to give you hope and a*
> *future."*
>
> JEREMIAH 29:11

> *Though you have made me see troubles, many and*
> *bitter, you will restore my life again.*
>
> PSALM 71:20

> *When I awake, I am still with you.*
>
> PSALM 139:18

*And provide for those who grieve in Zion—
to bestow on them a crown of beauty instead
of ashes, the oil of gladness instead of
mourning, and a garment of praise instead of a
spirit of despair.
They will be called oaks of righteousness, a
planting of the LORD for the display of his
splendor.*

ISAIAH 61:3

When we feel broken and useless, is there any hope?

*But he said to me, "My grace is sufficient
for you, for my power is made perfect in
weakness." Therefore I will boast all the
more gladly about my weaknesses, so that
Christ's power may rest on me. That is why,
for Christ's sake, I delight in weaknesses,
in insults, in hardships, in persecutions, in
difficulties. For when I am weak, then I am
strong.*

2 CORINTHIANS 12:9-10

HOW DOES THIS AFFECT ME???

Sins involving sex are not innocent dabblings in forbidden pleasures. Don't believe what is often portrayed in the media. Many songs and movie themes glorify rape and desensitize the listeners to sexual violence. They confuse and tear down the climate of respect, trust, and credibility that is so essential for solid marriages and secure children.

Become an overcomer, not just a survivor. Begin a

relationship with Jesus Christ! And as the Bible says, steer clear from anything that would promote or glorify any sexual perversions.

REBECCA JONES is a True Lies speaker.

self-image

GARY RIDGE

"Be what you is and not what you ain't. Cause if you ain't what you is, you is what you ain't." Although that saying would make your English teacher lose sleep at night, the message is clear. Stop pretending to be something you aren't.

Image can be very deceptive. Do you really think supermodels look covergirl beautiful without the aid of beauty tricks and computer enhancement? Do movie stars live perfect and glamorous lives? Sometimes, as we watch movies, videos, and television, we think we want to live the life of a superstar. We tend to compare ourselves with the models in magazines. Our self-image is attacked when compared to those seemingly perfect people. What we fail to realize is that those images are fake. Many have had numerous surgeries, and they diet constantly. Furthermore, photos are commonly touched up before they hit the page. After makeup, lighting, and the swift hand of an editor, anybody would look thin and toned. But that's not reality. Some actors have even commented publicly that they don't recognize themselves in photos. Just remember that they are out to sell you something. And the better they make it look, the more people buy it.

But sometimes the media's message hits a little closer to reality. Take the movie *Maid in Manhattan*, for example. Jennifer Lopez plays a single mom struggling to make a better life for herself and her son. It's a crazy love story about a maid who pretends to be a rich guest at the hotel where she works. She falls in love with a handsome rich guy who doesn't know that she is really the maid. Can she hide her secret or should she tell him who she really is? Will she lose him forever? Is her fake fairy-tale life worth the risk of being found out? Although a bit dramatic, this story is a good example of the consequences of trying to be something you aren't.

The problem is our concept of what makes us important. Unfortunately, some of us gather self-worth from our looks or accomplishments. We base our value on what others think of us. This is not what God intended. He desires that we see ourselves through His eyes. We are His beautiful creation, which He loves—just the way we are. This is our true identity. Don't let your friends, or even strangers, dictate how you live your life. Find your true self in God, and He will lead you the rest of the way.

WHAT DOES GOD SAY???

For we are God's workmanship, created in Christ Jesus to do good works, which God prepared in advance for us to do.

EPHESIANS 2:10

I praise you because I am fearfully and wonderfully made; your works are wonderful, I know that full well. My frame was not hidden from you when I was made in the secret place. When I was woven together in the depths of the earth, your eyes saw my unformed body. All the days ordained for me were written in your book before one of them came to be.

PSALM 139:14-16

God values you enough to pay the ultimate price for you.

You were bought at a price. Therefore honor
God with your body.

1 CORINTHIANS 6:20

God wants to use you no matter how untalented you think you are.

Moses said to the LORD, "O Lord, I have never
been eloquent, neither in the past nor since
you have spoken to your servant. I am slow
of speech and tongue." The LORD said to him,
"Who gave man his mouth? Who makes him deaf or
mute? Who gives him sight or makes him blind?
Is it not I, the LORD? Now go; I will help you
speak and will teach you what to say."

EXODUS 4:10-12

HOW DOES THIS AFFECT ME???

God fashioned you just the way He wanted you to be. He is proud of
you. Jesus gave His life just so you can be with Him for eternity.
Take some time to thank Him for creating and loving you just as
you are. And start living like a child of the King.

GARY RIDGE is a True Lies speaker.

sex

JONATHAN McKEE

God created sex. It is not only to be enjoyed, but it also serves
the very practical purpose of creating a family. God said to
Adam and Eve in the Garden of Eden, "Be fruitful and increase in
number; fill the earth and subdue it" (Genesis 1:28). In a world
before sin, there was no perversion of this God-given desire.

But of course, the fall of humankind caused all kinds of
problems. Adam and Eve were naked and ashamed, and childbirth
became painful. The selfishness of the first humans had lasting
consequences. God had given this great gift to enjoy, but it was
partially corrupted by self-pleasing people. To this day we are
still battling with a skewed understanding of sex and pleasure.

The Bible has many accounts of people who were messed up
sexually. Some repented and were forgiven. Others paid severe
consequences. King David, a man after God's own heart, spotted a
woman taking a bath on her roof one hot summer night. That led
to a sexual encounter and adultery. She ended up pregnant. David
tried to cover up the affair by having her husband killed in
battle (2 Samuel 11). David made things much worse by not facing
his sin.

So sexual immorality can start with just one look. Followed
by a long, lustful stare, a look can lead down a road of sexual
immorality before you know it. When taken out of the original
context of marriage, sex can only lead to pain, shame, and serious
consequences. The ramifications can even affect intimacy with
your future wife or husband. We were never meant to carry such
baggage into marriage. Keep yourself pure. Then you will be able
to fully understand the benefits of God's original plan.

Here are a few verses about God's original plan for sex.

One form of abusing sex is fornication, having sex outside of marriage.

The body is not meant for sexual immorality, but for the Lord, and the Lord for the body. . . . Do you not know that he who unites himself with a prostitute is one with her in body? . . . Flee from sexual immorality. All other sins a man commits are outside his body, but he who sins sexually sins against his own body. Do you not know that your body is a temple of the Holy Spirit, who is in you, whom you have received from God? You are not your own; you were bought at a price. Therefore honor God with your body.

1 CORINTHIANS 6:13, 16, 18-20

But among you there must not be even a hint of sexual immorality, or of any kind of impurity, or of greed, because these are improper for God's holy people.

EPHESIANS 5:3

It is God's will that you should be sanctified: that you should avoid sexual immorality; that each of you should learn to control his own body in a way that is holy and honorable, not in passionate lust like the heathen, who do not know God.

1 THESSALONIANS 4:3-5

Another form of abusing sex is adultery (having sex with someone else while married).

> *"You shall not commit adultery."*
>
> Exodus 20:14

> *But a man who commits adultery lacks judgment; whoever does so destroys himself.*
>
> Proverbs 6:32

> *Marriage should be honored by all, and the marriage bed kept pure, for God will judge the adulterer and all the sexually immoral.*
>
> Hebrews 13:4

Lust is just as bad as the action.

> *"You have heard that it was said, 'Do not commit adultery.' But I tell you that anyone who looks at a woman lustfully has already committed adultery with her in his heart."*
>
> Matthew 5:27-28

HOW DOES THIS AFFECT ME???

Are we getting the picture here? God is saying that we shouldn't be sleeping around, toying with sex, and trying to push the boundaries. Stop asking, "How far is too far?" God designed sex for us to enjoy with one person, for life, in the commitment of marriage. Honestly, it's the only godly way to pursue our natural desires.

Making good choices starts with knowing the truth. Unfortunately, immediate pleasure often gets in the way. We need to see God's plan for sex clearly and understand that He is looking out for us, offering us a better future. If you've been sexually active, ask for His forgiveness today. He's waiting for you. Make a fresh start and remain pure until marriage. God will bless you, your marriage, and your sex life.

JONATHAN MCKEE is a national speaker. For more info, log on to www.TheSource4YM.com.

suicide
ANDY JANNING

42

I've spent a lot of time working the phones at a crisis and suicide center. Night after night, I've listened to strangers on the phone tell me how slowly bleeding to death, swallowing dozens of pills, or putting a bullet through their forehead would somehow be better than the lives they are leading.

"I've already taken half a bottle of sleeping pills because I don't want to wake up anymore."

"I've got a knife to my wrist right now."

"Give me a reason not to blow my head off tonight."

People are hurting, and more and more are turning to suicide—especially young people. Suicide rates among youth (ages fifteen to twenty-four) have increased more than 200 percent in the last fifty years. Every two hours a person under the age of twenty-five kills himself or herself. At least two-thirds of those victims suffered from depression and believed that suicide was an easy escape from their problems. I've read too many stories of young lives cut short to think that suicide is a legitimate solution. It's really a lie from Satan himself.

If you feel your life is slipping out of control and death is the only way out, don't reach for a gun, a bottle, or a knife. Reach instead for those who are trained to help. Reach for a Bible and read how Jesus overcame the same problems you may be struggling with today. He walked this earth as a human and faced all of the same temptations and frustrations as everyone else. He wants to help—if only you'll ask.

Crisis counselors are trained to keep the caller focused on "living cues"—people and situations in the caller's life that remind them about the positives of life, not the negatives.

God's Word is filled with living cues.

> *"I have told you these things, so that in me you may have peace. In this world you will have trouble. But take heart! I have overcome the world."*
>
> JOHN 16:33

The world can close in around you, but it can't defeat you.

> *We are hard pressed on every side, but not crushed; perplexed, but not in despair; persecuted, but not abandoned; struck down, but not destroyed.*
>
> 2 CORINTHIANS 4:8-9

Even when you think you can't go on, God will always sustain you.

> *He gives strength to the weary and increases the power of the weak. Even youths grow tired and weary, and young men stumble and fall; but those who hope in the LORD will renew their strength. They will soar on wings like eagles; they will run and not grow weary, they will walk and not be faint.*
>
> ISAIAH 40:29-31

God has an awesome plan for your life.

> *"For I know the plans I have for you,"*
> *declares the LORD, "plans to prosper you and*
> *not to harm you, plans to give you hope and a*
> *future."*
>
> JEREMIAH 29:11

Were there any suicides in the Bible?

Yes, but most were non-Christians in distress. Look up the following in God's Word: 1 Samuel 31:4; 2 Samuel 17:23; 1 Kings 16:18; 1 Chronicles 10:4–5; Matthew 27:5; Acts 1:18.

> *The jailer woke up, and when he saw the*
> *prison doors open, he drew his sword and was*
> *about to kill himself because he thought*
> *the prisoners had escaped. But Paul shouted,*
> *"Don't harm yourself! We are all here!" The*
> *jailer called for lights, rushed in and fell*
> *trembling before Paul and Silas. He then*
> *brought them out and asked, "Sirs, what must*
> *I do to be saved?" They replied, "Believe in*
> *the Lord Jesus, and you will be saved—you and*
> *your household." Then they spoke the word*
> *of the Lord to him and to all the others*
> *in his house. At that hour of the night the*
> *jailer took them and washed their wounds;*
> *then immediately he and all his family were*
> *baptized. The jailer brought them into his*
> *house and set a meal before them; he was*
> *filled with joy because he had come to believe*
> *in God—he and his whole family.*
>
> ACTS 16:27-34

Who is behind suicide? I'll give you one guess. Jesus calls him the thief in the following verse. Yes, it's Satan himself.

"The thief comes only to steal and kill and destroy; I have come that they may have life, and have it to the full."

JOHN 10:10

HOW DOES THIS AFFECT ME???

"If I commit suicide, will I go to hell?" That's a good question, but probably the wrong one to ask. (There are varying thoughts on this issue in the Church.) Instead, ask, "Why would a Christian kill himself or herself?" Suicide hurts everyone around those who kill themselves, including God. He has a plan for your life. Don't play God and decide to take your own life.

Have you considered suicide? If you have and now you're reading this, you're probably looking for a reason to live—and not a reason to die. There are people who can help. Call 1-800-SUICIDE or 1-800-999-9999 and speak privately about your feelings. Pass this number on to anyone who may need it. Remember, Jesus said, "Come to me, all you who are weary and burdened, and I will give you rest" (Matthew 11:28). Take comfort in these words. Your life depends on them!

ANDY JANNING is a True Lies speaker.

tattoos and piercing

JEFFREY SHICKS

I've been a police officer, a youth leader, and am a parent. I've seen it all. No matter where you go, people love to express themselves. They use music, drama, sports, clothing, and even tattoos and piercings. But why choose something so permanent as tattoos? For some it's a display of their convictions or religious beliefs or rebellion toward authority figures. Others just follow the current trend. As a police officer, I was trained to notice any tats that were gang or violence related. These lifelong symbols let the world know who an individual is and what he or she believes in.

Some teens desperately need to feel loved—so much so that they agree to do painful things they will regret later in life. Like placing an extremely hot paper clip shaped into a symbol to their body to create a scar known as a brand.

More and more teens are going with the Goth look. They dress all in black, wear dark makeup, and riddle their bodies with piercing after piercing. A lack of love may cause people to go to extremes to be noticed.

I confess I have one of my ears pierced. I did it at the request of my son on his thirteenth birthday. He wanted us both to get our ears pierced at the same time as father and son. So why not? It's a fun display of our love for each other.

These outward expressions can be good or bad. The real question is, "Why get a tattoo or piercing?" An honest answer will determine whether it is God's will or not.

During the time of Moses, those who were worshiping other gods or idols would cut themselves and pierce their bodies. They would also tattoo themselves with markings signifying their beliefs. The tattoos indicated what idols they worshiped. When God lead His people out of Egypt, He desired that their worship and faith be rooted in a personal relationship with their Creator. He didn't want rituals and rules. He wanted their hearts. So in Leviticus 19 He prohibited His believers from altering their bodies in this way. He wanted them to worship Him through their lifestyles. They would show the joy of their salvation by their love and dedication—not tattoos and piercings.

Is my body important to God? Yes, it is God's temple.

> *Do you not know that your body is a temple of the Holy Spirit, who is in you, whom you have received from God? You are not your own; you were bought at a price. Therefore honor God with your body.*
>
> 1 CORINTHIANS 6:19-20

> *I urge you, brothers, in view of God's mercy, to offer your bodies as living sacrifices, holy and pleasing to God—this is your spiritual act of worship. Do not conform any longer to the pattern of this world, but be transformed by the renewing of your mind.*
>
> ROMANS 12:1-2

Is what others see in my actions important?

> *Do not let anyone look down on you because you are young, but set an example for the believers in speech, in life, in love, in faith and in purity. . . . Be diligent in these matters; give yourself wholly to them, so that everyone may see your progress. Watch your life and doctrine closely. Persevere in them, because if you do, you will save both yourself and your hearers.*
>
> 1 TIMOTHY 4:12, 15-16

Should we be more concerned about outward appearance or the heart?

> *"Man looks at the outward appearance, but the LORD looks at the heart."*
>
> 1 SAMUEL 16:7

HOW DOES THIS AFFECT ME???

So, why do you want a tattoo or piercing? What's the real reason? Is it a sign of your faith? Or is it to fit in with a certain group of friends? What do your parents think? Like it or not, it matters. We are commanded to honor our fathers and mothers. If they say no, then you will have to wait until you're a little older for that tattoo.

Why not find another way to express yourself? Dress a certain way, drive a different car, or pick up a fun new hobby. You have many options. And it's a lot easier to change your clothes than it is to repair some type of body modification.

I'm not going to tell you whether tattoos and piercings are

right or wrong. The Bible doesn't say anything about this type of self-expression (outside of pagan worship). So it's up to you to ask the hard questions, be honest with your answers, pray about it, and listen for God's direction.

JEFFREY SHICKS is a True Lies speaker and director of The Bridge.

temptation and self-control

ROGER PALMER

What's your greatest weakness? Is it lust, pride, gossip, anger, or fear? It could be just about anything. We all have certain areas in our lives in which we struggle. We must continually submit those temptations to the Father in order to walk in obedience to Him.

Well, you're not the only one who is tempted. Even Jesus was tempted. God has given all of us a free will. We get to choose how to live, what to believe, and whom to follow. That means we have to make choices—daily.

The ongoing battle between good and evil is played out daily in the lives of Christians. The little temptations that we encounter along the way are just a part of the war for our hearts. We can't fight the battle alone. Whether we are new or mature believers, we need to fully submit to the Lord. And when we do, He gives us the power to succeed. His strength gives us endurance.

Take a look at your life. Are you living for God? Think about your friends, entertainment, dating life, jokes, and overall attitude. Are you making the right choices? If you're not sure, just pray about it. God is eager to lead you down the right path. Just ask. It's not easy, but your very soul hangs in the balance.

WHAT DOES GOD SAY???

Do not be afraid if you are facing temptations. Read and study the following verses and see what the strength of the Lord can do in and through you.

Blessed is the man who perseveres under trial, because when he has stood the test, he will receive the crown of life that God has promised to those who love him. When tempted, no one should say, "God is tempting me." For God cannot be tempted by evil, nor does he tempt anyone; but each one is tempted when, by his own evil desire, he is dragged away and enticed. Then, after desire has conceived, it gives birth to sin; and sin, when it is full-grown, gives birth to death.

JAMES 1:12-15

The Lord knows how to rescue godly men from trials.

2 PETER 2:9

Jesus understands our temptation. He was tempted just like us.

We do not have a high priest who is unable to sympathize with our weaknesses, but we have one who has been tempted in every way, just as we are—yet was without sin.

HEBREWS 4:15

We can overcome temptation.

No temptation has seized you except what is common to man. And God is faithful; he will not let you be tempted beyond what you can bear. But when you are tempted, he will also provide a way out so that you can stand up under it.

1 CORINTHIANS 10:13

We can overcome temptation by prayer and by knowing and applying God's Word.

"Watch and pray so that you will not fall into temptation. The spirit is willing, but the body is weak."

Matthew 26:41

How can a young man keep his way pure? By living according to your word.

Psalm 119:9

HOW DOES THIS AFFECT ME???

You will be tempted. Jesus comforted His followers by saying, "In this world you will have trouble. But take heart! I have overcome the world" (John 16:33). Know that you will stumble from time to time. When you do, ask for forgiveness, brush yourself off, and move forward.

You must choose daily. Your decisions will be governed by either the Holy Spirit or yourself. There is no in between. David told God in Psalm 119:11, "I have hidden your word in my heart that I might not sin against you." If you put God's Word in your heart regularly, you will have the ability to have victory over temptation. So start out each day by praying, reading the Bible, and deciding whom you will serve when your feet hit your bedroom floor.

ROGER PALMER is a True Lies speaker.

176

taming the tongue

ROGER PALMER

A young man stood in the middle of a classroom, nervously holding a handgun. He was a good student, but he was a little overweight and quiet. He didn't have many friends, and he kept to himself. He didn't play sports or a musical instrument and didn't have any other hobby to pursue. And of course, he was constantly picked on. He was shoved, teased, and laughed at every time he came to school. He was sick and tired. He just couldn't take it anymore. He didn't know any other way out.

The other students fell into two categories. One group joked and made fun of him. The other group sat by and watched it happen. They did nothing. As some publicly destroyed him, others remained silent. No one ever reached out to him. No one cared.

Our words are very powerful. The tongue may be one of the smallest muscles in the body, but it throws a powerful punch. It can make others feel loved or tear them down word by word. It can affect someone's life and death.

That boy standing in the classroom didn't turn his weapon on other classmates. He pointed it directly at himself and ended it all. A promising young life—wasted. His life didn't have to end that way. If only one person had reached out to him. Just one friend or even a few kind words from a stranger could have made a difference. There are many others like him in our midst. You may be like him. Or you may be the bully, or the quiet guy who stands by and lets the harassment happen. Think about your words. Consider their impact on those around you. Use them wisely!

*Do not let any unwholesome talk come out of
your mouths, but only what is helpful for
building others up according to their needs,
that it may benefit those who listen.*

EPHESIANS 4:29

*Let your conversation be always full of grace,
seasoned with salt, so that you may know how
to answer everyone.*

COLOSSIANS 4:6

*If anyone considers himself religious and yet
does not keep a tight rein on his tongue,
he deceives himself and his religion is
worthless.*

JAMES 1:26

*"But the things that come out of the mouth
come from the heart, and these make a man
'unclean.'"*

MATTHEW 15:18

*But now you must rid yourselves of all such
things as these: anger, rage, malice, slander,
and filthy language from your lips.*

COLOSSIANS 3:8

HOW DOES THIS AFFECT ME???

Do you remember the saying **"Sticks and stones may break my
bones, but words will never hurt me"**? What was the person who
wrote that thinking? Words do have the power to hurt and scar.

Proverbs 18:21 says, "The tongue has the power of life and death." Your tongue has the power to speak life—or death—to others.

James 3:5–10 says:

> Likewise the tongue is a small part of the body, but it makes great boasts. Consider what a great forest is set on fire by a small spark. The tongue also is a fire, a world of evil among the parts of the body. It corrupts the whole person, sets the whole course of his life on fire, and is itself set on fire by hell. All kinds of animals, birds, reptiles and creatures of the sea are being tamed and have been tamed by man, but no man can tame the tongue. It is a restless evil, full of deadly poison. With the tongue we praise our Lord and Father, and with it we curse men, who have been made in God's likeness. Out of the same mouth come praise and cursing. My brothers, this should not be.

We should be very careful about the words we use. Are we uplifting someone in one breath and tearing down someone else in the next? Do praises or cursing come out of your mouth? How will you use your tongue today?

ROGER PALMER is a True Lies speaker.

thug life

LG WISE

On a typical hot summer day close to the Fourth of July, I walked
down the streets of Brooklyn, New York. My neighborhood was
called "Do or Die." Either you were doing or you were dead.

Out of nowhere a red Jeep Cherokee pulled up next to me.
Five guys jumped out. They were the same guys I had robbed just
weeks before. With disgust on their faces, they called me by
my street name, Shorty. They said, "You should have killed us
when you had the chance!" These were the guys who had killed
my cousin, so I knew I was facing death. They grabbed me, picked
me up, and body-slammed me in the middle of the street. They
kicked me in the face and head with steel-toed boots. They beat
me so badly that I struggled to stay awake. The leader of the
crew got a steel trash can from the side of the street and beat
me in the back of my head until it split open. Their mission was
to kill me.

The leader told one of the guys to "get the .38 and smoke him."
While one guy went for the gun, the other guys jumped in the Jeep,
pulled around the block, and waited. He put the .38 in my face
and cocked it—but he didn't pull the trigger. I was scared and
confused.

All I could do as I lay there in the street, beaten and
bleeding, was pray. My whole life flashed before me. I thought of
the choices that had lead me to this point. I wanted to be a thug. I
thought it was cool. But I was getting ready to die a very painful
death. That wasn't cool. I didn't want to die young like so many of
my friends. I cried out for help.

Blessings crown the head of the righteous, but violence overwhelms the mouth of the wicked.

PROVERBS 10:6

Stay away from a foolish man, for you will not find knowledge on his lips.

PROVERBS 14:7

Fools mock at making amends for sin, but goodwill is found among the upright.

PROVERBS 14:9

The mouth of the wicked gushes evil.
The LORD is far from the wicked.

PROVERBS 15:28-29

There are six things the LORD hates, seven that are detestable to him: haughty eyes, a lying tongue, hands that shed innocent blood, a heart that devises wicked schemes, feet that are quick to rush into evil, a false witness who pours out lies, and a man who stirs up dissension among brothers.

PROVERBS 6:16-19

HOW DOES THIS AFFECT ME???

I was granted another chance. Instead of pulling the trigger, the thug uncocked the gun and ran. I was able to escape. But there are many others who don't get a second opportunity in life.

I know through my own life experiences that one bad choice can put you on the wrong path and lead you into a lifestyle of wrong choices. Before you know it, you're at the wrong destination, a place you probably never meant to be. Don't buy into the image of thug life. It's not glamorous or cool. It's tragic and deadly.

LG WISE is a rap artist.

video games

ANDY JANNING

"Bro, I had a great day yesterday! I had sex with a prostitute then beat her to death to get my money back. I flirted with strippers and saw them dance topless after riding my BMX bike. After that I spent a few hours shooting people in the head with a high-powered rifle. I urinated on one of the dead bodies and even kicked one of my victim's heads down the street like a soccer ball. Finally, I shot myself in the head just to get the day over with. And, believe it or not, it was fun!"

This is definitely not the kind of day you'd want to tell God about. But this is exactly how millions of teens spend their day when they play some of today's most popular video games, such as Grand Theft Auto 3, BMX XXX, Postal 2, Halo, and Hitman 2. The violence, gore, and sexuality in these games are brought to you in stunning detail, such as chunks of brain that splatter on a wall when you shoot a victim or the bare breasts of a stripper who dances for you when you "win." Some say these are just games— just harmless fun to escape from the world. Those people are flat-out wrong.

In 2002 researchers at Indiana University came to a shocking conclusion about video games and brain activity. They found that playing violent video games resulted in *significantly decreased brain activity* in the area that controls reasoning, intelligence, and impulse control. That decrease was most apparent in those who played for several hours a day. According to Carol Rumack, a doctor of radiology and pediatrics at the University of Colorado, the study suggests that repeated exposure to violent video games is "desensitizing the brain. The result is that the person can no longer understand the real effects of violence."

192

Numerous studies have been done, including one by the American Medical Association that says violent video games make children and teens more violent. If you're hooked on the challenge of a good game, try playing nonviolent ones such as Madden Football, Nascar and other racing games. They do exist; you just have to look for them.

WHAT DOES GOD SAY???

God wants our thought life to be pure.

> Nor should there be obscenity, foolish talk or coarse joking, which are out of place, but rather thanksgiving. . . . Let no one deceive you with empty words, for because of such things God's wrath comes on those who are disobedient. Therefore do not be partners with them.
>
> EPHESIANS 5:4, 6-7

When you fill your life with violent images, they can overwhelm you.

> The mouth of the righteous is a fountain of life, but violence overwhelms the mouth of the wicked.
>
> PROVERBS 10:11

Choose to keep your mind and life focused on God. And remember, the Bible is clear that just thinking about sex or violence, like acting it out in a game, is just as bad as committing the act.

> "But I tell you that anyone who looks at a woman lustfully has already committed adultery with her in his heart."
>
> MATTHEW 5:28

> *Finally, brothers, whatever is true, whatever is noble, whatever is right, whatever is pure, whatever is lovely, whatever is admirable—if anything is excellent or praiseworthy—think about such things.*
>
> PHILIPPIANS 4:8

HOW DOES THIS AFFECT ME???

First person shooter video games are killing simulators teaching a generation of children and teens how to kill. The U.S. Army and some police academies use the same video game technology to train their soldiers and officers.

Our actions speak loudly. When Christians play video games filled with violence and sexuality, we look like hypocrites because our actions go against whom we claim to be. Don't be lured in by the graphics and fast-paced action. It isn't worth your time, energy, and money.

ANDY JANNING is a True Lies speaker.

violence

JEREMY BEEBE

I grew up as a missionary kid. In 1986 we moved from the Solomon Islands to the small nation of Palau, just south of Guam. Being a missionary family wasn't easy, but we knew that God had called us. Every member of my family shared in the mission to reach other nations with the gospel.

We had our scares. While in the Solomon Islands, my dad's life had been threatened, and we had survived earthquakes and even a major hurricane. But Palau proved to be our biggest challenge. Just six weeks after we arrived, our home was broken into during the night. Three men proceeded to torture us for an entire night. My dad was stabbed, hit over the head with a shotgun, and left for dead. My mom and my sister, who was only eleven, were beaten and raped. The men held a gun to my head multiple times threatening to kill me.

In the early morning, my dad, sister, and I were able to escape. Rescuers found my mom hours later. We survived. We had lived through the worst night of our lives. But God had a plan—and it wasn't to die at the hands of our attackers. Months later we watched as these men stood trial. As we learned the details, we found out that they had simply copied what they had seen in a few movies.

Now, nearly seventeen years later, we are all healthy and serving God in full-time ministry. My parents are pastoring an amazing church in Washington and travel to Serbia several times a year. There they minister to refugees who have survived the rape camps from recent wars. My sister has been married for six years to a chaplain in the U.S. Army, and they have two young boys. I travel and speak, sharing my story with thousands across America.

The enemy may have won a battle, but he did not win the war. God has turned what was intended for evil into good.

The first recorded act of violence in the Bible is Cain's killing of Abel in Genesis. But it didn't stop there. Read these verses that talk about violence.

Now the earth was corrupt in God's sight and was full of violence. . . . So God said to Noah, "I am going to put an end to all people, for the earth is filled with violence because of them. I am surely going to destroy both them and the earth."

GENESIS 6:11, 13

The LORD examines the righteous, but the wicked and those who love violence his soul hates.

PSALM 11:5

Do not set foot on the path of the wicked or walk in the way of evil men. . . .
They eat the bread of wickedness and drink the wine of violence.

PROVERBS 4:14, 17

The mouth of the righteous is a fountain of life, but violence overwhelms the mouth of the wicked.

PROVERBS 10:11

"The thief comes only to steal and kill and destroy; I have come that they may have life, and have it to the full."

JOHN 10:10

HOW DOES THIS AFFECT ME???

Violence overwhelms our society. Countless violent acts are committed every day throughout the United States and around the world. We all have experienced it. We have been affected by the Columbine school shootings, the September 11, 2001, terrorist attacks, and crimes committed in our own neighborhoods. Unfortunately, the violence is not likely to stop, for we are a fallen people with a heritage of sin that dates as far back as Adam and Eve. Violence is the result of Satan's rule over this world and human lives.

God calls us not to fear violence but to keep doing the work He has for us. First John 4:4 says, "You, dear children, are from God and have overcome them, because the one who is in you is greater than the one who is in the world." As Christians, we face the challenge of being different—set apart from the ways of this world.

Become aware of the effects of violence around you. Recognize the desensitizing effect of certain activities. Discern what is good for you to watch, listen to, and play. Choose to make a difference. Never forget that God is greater than the one who is in the world!

JEREMY BEEBE is a True Lies speaker.

witnessing

ROGER PALMER

50

Witnessing. It's one of those words that can make us cringe. I love telling people about my relationship with Christ, but I still get butterflies every time. Maybe I'm scared of rejection or that something will go wrong or I won't be able to answer someone's questions. Maybe it's all of those fears wrapped up together.

I began sharing my story as a new believer at age nineteen. I remember working on a class project in the library with a friend. I felt that I needed to tell him about my relationship with Christ. My stomach was doing somersaults and my hands were sweating. Somehow I opened my mouth and began asking him questions about his spiritual life. I shared about my own search for Christ and told him how God had found and changed me. Before I knew it, I was asking him if he had ever wanted a relationship with Christ. He said no. But to my surprise, he said he wanted to start a relationship with Christ right then. *Wow!* Was I shocked! We prayed, and he invited Christ into his life. My friend had a life-changing experience right there in the middle of the library. He said *yes* to Christ.

That day changed my life as well. I realized the life-changing power of the truth of Jesus.

WHAT DOES GOD SAY???

Don't be afraid!

For God did not give us a spirit of timidity, but a spirit of power, of love and of self-discipline.

So do not be ashamed to testify about our Lord.

2 TIMOTHY 1:7-8

Witnessing is a good thing and helps you be active in your faith.

I pray that you may be active in sharing your faith, so that you will have a full understanding of every good thing we have in Christ.

PHILEMON 1:6

We can save a person from death, which in this verse means spiritual death or hell.

Remember this: Whoever turns a sinner from the error of his way will save him from death and cover over a multitude of sins.

JAMES 5:20

Be merciful to those who doubt; snatch others from the fire and save them.

JUDE 22-23

In the Great Commission, Jesus commanded us to share our faith with others. These are some of His last recorded words:

"All authority in heaven and on earth has been given to me. Therefore go and make disciples of all nations, baptizing them in the name of the Father and of the Son and of the Holy Spirit, and teaching them to obey everything I have commanded you."

MATTHEW 28:18-20

HOW DOES THIS AFFECT ME???

You know the cure for sin and the key to heaven and eternity with God. Don't you think it's time to do something about it? You don't have to carry a sign around that says, "You are going to hell." Just live your life as a Christian, and people will notice and ask questions. You can also begin sharing your story in a very loving and nonconfrontational way. You don't have to cram it down people's throats. Your responsibility is to share Christ. God is the one who will touch their hearts and draw them to Him. It's as easy as that.

Pray for the lost every day. Keep a list, and don't stop praying for them until they are believers. If you need a little help, go back and reread the introduction to this book. Take a chance and watch God change the lives of people around you!

ROGER PALMER is a True Lies speaker. Additional help from Kris and Kristin Howell.

E-mail Phil Chalmers at Phil@PhilChalmers.com
Be sure to visit his Web sites: PhilChalmers.com and TeenKillers.com